PRAISE FOR
DATA STRATEGY

'Algorithms will control every aspect of our lives. This book is the 2017 how-to guide to take advantage of data to out-think, out-compete and out-perform.' **Henrik von Scheel, Advisory Board Member, Google**

'*Data Strategy* isn't just for data people. Bernard Marr shows that a data strategy deserves attention on the same level as a company's marketing, customer, product, and talent strategies. In my experience, a data strategy is critical to the success of all of these efforts. I believe Marr's book is a valuable starting point for developing your data strategy. I found it brought together a number of lessons I've learned. If you've never developed a data strategy, it's worth reading twice.' **David Purdy, Data Scientist, Uber**

'If you're a person in charge of data strategy for your company, but still struggle to articulate the size of the task and subsequent reward for building a data-driven culture, this book can help provide a well-rounded pulse on the change that is happening in business today, and arm you with the beginning of a structure to tackle it.' **Jake Williams, Retail Strategy, Amazon**

'A complex topic with many strands made simple – packed with accessible examples from global household brands, right down to smaller chain stores. Bernard Marr's latest book on data strategy covers many critical elements for anyone trying to get to grips with the data-driven economy in an accessible, conversational style that means that this book will be an interesting read for those who wish to know more about how the human race is evolving supported by data and devices, and what they might need to think about within their own organization to align with this agenda.' **Gareth Mitchell-Jones, Cognitive Systems, IBM**

'A clear, concise and exciting road map for maximizing value from data in today's hyper-competitive business landscape.' **Ralph Blore, Leader, Central Analytics, Visa**

'As we enter the Fourth Industrial Revolution, Bernard Marr tells us that it will be those companies that view data as a strategic asset that will survive and

Data Strategy

How to profit from a world of big data, analytics and the internet of things

Bernard Marr

KoganPage

Publisher's note

Every possible effort has been made to ensure that the information contained in this book is accurate at the time of going to press, and the publishers and authors cannot accept responsibility for any errors or omissions, however caused. No responsibility for loss or damage occasioned to any person acting, or refraining from action, as a result of the material in this publication can be accepted by the editor, the publisher or the author.

First published in Great Britain and the United States in 2017 by Kogan Page Limited

2nd Floor, 45 Gee Street	c/o Martin P Hill Consulting	4737/23 Ansari Road
London	122 W 27th St, 10th Floor	Daryaganj
EC1V 3RS	New York, NY 10001	New Delhi 110002
United Kingdom	USA	India

www.koganpage.com

© Bernard Marr, 2017

ISBN   978 0 7494 7985 5
E-ISBN 978 0 7494 7986 2

British Library Cataloguing-in-Publication Data

A CIP record for this book is available from the British Library.

Library of Congress Control Number

2017001789

Typeset by Integra Software Services, Pondicherry
Print production managed by Jellyfish
Printed and bound by CPI Group (UK) Ltd, Croydon CR0 4YY

*This book is dedicated to the four people
that are my world:*

*My wife, Claire, and our three children,
Sophia, James and Oliver.*

CONTENTS

About the author xi
Acknowledgements xiii

01 Why every business is now a data business 1
The astonishing growth of big data and the Internet of Things 1
A brave new (data-driven) world 2
Are we nearing artificial intelligence? 5
How data is revolutionizing the world of business 7
Every business must become a data business 16
Endnotes 19

02 Deciding your strategic data needs 21
Using data to make better business decisions 22
Using data to improve your operations 25
Transforming your business model: data as a business asset 31
The importance of the *right* data, not *all* data 33
Making a strong business case for data 35
Endnotes 36

03 Using data to improve your business decisions 37
Setting out your key business questions 37
Questions related to your customers, markets and competition 40
Visualizing and communicating insights from data 50
Endnote 55

04 Using data to improve your business operations 57
Optimizing your operational processes with data 58
Using data to improve your customer offering 66
Endnotes 71

05 Monetizing your data 73
Increasing the value of your organization 74
When data itself is the core business asset 74

When the value lies in a company's ability to work with data 77
Selling data to customers or interested parties 78
Understanding the value of user-generated data 82

06   Sourcing and collecting data 85
Understanding the different types of data 86
Taking a look at newer types of data 93
Gathering your internal data 96
Accessing external data 97
When the data you want doesn't exist 99
Endnote 100

07   Turning data into insights   101
How analytics has evolved 102
Looking at the different types of analytics 103
Advanced analytics: machine learning, deep learning and cognitive computing 114
Combining analytics for maximum success 117

08   Creating the technology and data infrastructure 119
'Big data as a service': the one-stop solution for businesses? 120
Collecting data 122
Storing data 124
Analysing and processing data 129
Providing access to data 132
Endnote 135

09   Building data competencies in your organization 137
The big data skill shortage, and what it means for your business 138
Building internal skills and competencies 140
Outsourcing your data analysis 145
Endnotes 150

10   Ensuring your data doesn't become a liability: data governance   151
Considering data ownership and privacy 152
Tackling data security 159
Practising good data governance 163
Endnotes 165

11   Executing and revisiting your data strategy 167
Putting the data strategy into practice 167
Creating a data culture 172
Revisiting the data strategy 173
Endnotes 179

Index 181

To accompany the book, the author has prepared an additional online resource, *Beyond the Big Data Buzz*, which can be found at: **www.koganpage.com/beyond-the-big-data-buzz**.

ABOUT THE AUTHOR

Bernard Marr is an internationally bestselling business author, keynote speaker and strategic adviser to companies and governments. He is one of the world's most highly respected voices when it comes to data in business and has been recognized by LinkedIn as one of the world's top five business influencers.

Bernard is a regular contributor to the World Economic Forum, writes regular columns for *Forbes* and LinkedIn Pulse and his expert comments have been featured on TV and radio (eg BBC News, Sky News and BBC World) as well as in high-profile publications including *The Times*, *Financial Times*, *CFO Magazine* and *The Wall Street Journal*.

He has written a number of seminal books and hundreds of high-profile reports and articles, including the international bestsellers *Big Data in Practice: How 45 successful companies used big data analytics to deliver extraordinary results*; *Big Data: Using SMART big data, analytics and metrics to make better decisions and improve performance*; *Key Business Analytics: The 60+ business analysis tools every manager needs to know*; *The Intelligent Company*; and *Big Data for Small Business* in the 'For Dummies' series.

Bernard has worked with and advised many of the world's best-known organizations including Accenture, Astra Zeneca, Bank of England, Barclays, BP, Cisco, DHL, Fujitsu, Gartner, HSBC, IBM, Mars, Ministry of Defence, Microsoft, NATO, Oracle, The Home Office, NHS, Orange, Tetley, T-Mobile, Toyota, Royal Air Force, SAP, Shell, the United Nations and Walmart, among many others.

If you would like to talk to Bernard about any advisory work, speaking engagements or training needs then you can contact him at www.ap-institute.com or via e-mail at bernard.marr@ap-institute.com.

You can also follow @bernardmarr on Twitter, where he regularly shares his ideas, or connect with him on LinkedIn where he writes a regular blog.

ACKNOWLEDGEMENTS

I feel extremely lucky to work in a field that is so innovative and fast moving and I feel privileged that I am able to work with companies and government organizations across all sectors and industries on new and better ways to use data to deliver real value – this work allows me to learn every day and a book like this wouldn't have been possible without it.

I would like to acknowledge the many people who have helped me get to where I am today; all the great individuals in the companies I have worked with who put their trust in me to help them and in return gave me so much new knowledge and experience. I must also thank everyone who has shared their thinking with me, either in person, in blog posts, in books or any other formats. Thank you for generously sharing all the material I absorb every day! I am also lucky enough to personally know many of the key thinkers and thought leaders in the field and I hope you all know how much I value your inputs and our exchanges.

Finally, I must thank my editorial and publishing team for all your help and support. Taking any book from idea to publication is a challenging process and I really appreciate your input and help – thank you Claire, David, Amy and Lucy.

Why every business is now a data business

01

Data is changing our world and the way we live and work at an unprecedented rate. Depending on your viewpoint, we're either at the start of something incredibly exciting or we're entering a terrifying Big Brother era where our every move can be tracked – and even predicted (both sides have a point). Business leaders and managers, however, have little time for data scepticism. Data is already revolutionizing the way companies operate and it will become increasingly critical to organizations in the coming years. Those companies that view data as a strategic asset are the ones that will survive and thrive. With the massive growth in big data and the Internet of Things, plus rapidly evolving methods for analysing data, the importance of data across every aspect of business will only increase.

The astonishing growth of big data and the Internet of Things

Every two days we create as much data as we did from the beginning of time until 2003. Every two days. And the amount of data we're creating continues to increase rapidly; by 2020, the amount of digital information available will have grown from about 5 zettabytes today to 50 zettabytes. Almost every action we take leaves a digital trail – browsing online, shopping in a bricks-and-mortar store with a credit card, sending an e-mail, taking a photograph, reading an online article, even walking down the street if you're carrying a mobile phone or there are CCTV cameras in the vicinity.

The term 'big data' refers to the collection of all that data and our ability to use it to our advantage across a wide range of areas, including business. Data in itself isn't a new invention. Going back even before computers and databases, we still used data to track actions and simplify processes – think of paper transaction records and archive files. Computers, and particularly spreadsheets and databases, gave us a way to store and organize data on a large scale, in an easily accessible way. Suddenly, information was available at the click of a mouse.

Until relatively recently, though, data was limited to spreadsheets or databases – and it was all very ordered and neat. Anything that wasn't easily organized into rows and columns was simply too difficult to work with and was ignored. Now, however, advances in storage and analytics mean that we can capture, store and work with many, many different types of data. As a result, data today can cover everything from spreadsheets to photos, videos, sound recordings, written text and sensor data.

There's no doubt that the sheer amount of data we're creating is, well, big. But, if I'm honest, I've never been entirely comfortable with the term 'big data'. It feels too simplistic to me, focusing on the volume of data rather than the incredible opportunities this data creates. I wish there was a better term to describe this huge shift in our technology, culture and world. That's why, in this book, I talk about 'data' in all senses, big and small – because it doesn't matter how much data you have, it's whether you use it successfully that counts.

A brave new (data-driven) world

Big data knows a lot about you. It goes way beyond Google knowing what you've searched for online and Facebook knowing who you're friends with. Your Internet service provider knows every website you've ever visited. Ever. Even in private browsing. Google knows your age and gender (even if you've never told them) and you can be sure they have a comprehensive profile of you and your interests, so they can decide what ads to show you. Facebook clearly knows who you're friends with and who you're in a relationship with. But did you know Facebook can also predict whether your relationship is going to last or, if you're single, when you're about to be in a relationship (and with whom)? Facebook can also tell how intelligent you are, based on an analysis of your 'likes'. (In case you're wondering, liking Curly Fries, Science, Mozart, Thunderstorms or The Daily Show predicted high intelligence, while likes for Harley Davidson, Lady Antebellum, and I Love Being a Mom predicted low intelligence.)

The police know where you're driving, certainly in the UK, where they have access to thousands of networked CCTV cameras across the country that scan number plates and take pictures of cars and their drivers. In the United States, many cities make similar use of traffic cameras. Your phone also knows how fast you're driving. For now, that information isn't shared with the police, but more and more insurance companies are starting to make use of smartphone data to deduce who is a safe driver and who's a riskier prospect.

Your grocery store loyalty card tracks the brands you like and collects mountains of information on your purchasing habits and preferences. Retailers use this data to personalize your shopping experience, but it can also be used to predict what else you might want to buy in future. In one well-known case, US retailer Target predicted a teenage girl was pregnant (based on her buying habits) and started sending her baby-related offers – the only problem was her own parents didn't yet know she was pregnant.

Big data powers much more than social media networks and coupon mailings, though. Its influence stretches to almost every aspect of modern life, from healthcare to space exploration, even to our political elections.

In an analytics-driven election campaign, for example, the focus is on targeting swing or undecided voters. After all, why waste time campaigning to those who are definitely going to vote for you, or those who never will in a million years? This technique was pioneered by the Obama campaign in 2012 when a team of over 100 data analysts were tasked with running over 66,000 computer simulations every day.

First, Obama's analysts collected and amalgamated all the data they could from voter registration data, donations, public records and bought-in third-party commercial data (including data mined from social media). Then everybody who had been identified was evaluated on their likelihood of voting for Obama, based on how well their data profile matched that of known supporters. Armed with their sophisticated demographic information, the team then launched targeted campaigns. These were aimed at increasing voter turnout and registration amongst sectors where the likelihood of backing their candidate was high, and influencing voter choice in sectors where the support metric indicated voters could go either way. This meant that targeted messages could be despatched – via e-mail, social media posts and browser display ads – depending on whether an individual needed to be convinced to register, vote, or pick the correct candidate.

In the years since then, all parties and most candidates have enthusiastically launched their own analytics strategies.

Big data is also helping to answer the question of whether there has ever been life on Mars. NASA's Jet Propulsion Laboratory, which runs the day-to-day mission planning for the Mars Rover spacecraft, is now using Elasticsearch technology (also used by companies like Netflix and Goldman Sachs) to process all of the data transmitted from the Rover craft during its four daily scheduled uploads. While mission-planning decisions used to be based on the previous day's data, the move to real-time analytics vastly speeds up the time in which decisions can be taken by mission control. Patterns and anomalies in the data sets can be spotted far more quickly, and correlations which could provide mission-critical insights are more likely to become apparent, leading to a greater rate of scientific discovery and less danger of malfunction or failure.

Even healthcare has not escaped the big data touch. For years, the basis of most medical research and discovery has been the collection and analysis of data: who gets sick, how they get sick and why. But now, with sensors in every smartphone and doctors able to share information across disciplines, the quantity and quality of the data available are greater than ever before, which means that the potential for breakthroughs and change is growing just as exponentially. Smartphones and other popular smart devices including Jawbone, Fitbit and others, now have the capacity to help people track their progress towards a healthier lifestyle. Apps and devices to help track and monitor chronic ailments like diabetes, Parkinson's and heart disease are also being developed.

The medical industry already collects a huge amount of data, but it's often siloed in individual doctors' offices, hospitals and clinics. Unifying that data – and combining it with patient-collected data from smart devices – is the industry's next big hurdle to overcome. Healthcare providers are already focusing on digitizing patient records and ensuring access to one set of records across the healthcare system. Pattern recognition software is already being used to aid diagnostics. So far, certain algorithms are proving as effective or more effective than human diagnosticians in spotting cancers in test results. There is incredible potential here for catching more diseases at earlier stages, and thus increasing the likelihood of treatment success. Big data is also being used to track, analyse and treat epidemics across the world, including Ebola and Zika.

All this is just the tip of the iceberg, and data volumes will only continue to grow. More often than not, when we sign up to a new product or service, whether it's a fitness tracker or a store loyalty card, we're happily giving access to our personal data – in return for benefits like improving our fitness or collecting points towards a free coffee. As more companies tap into the possibilities of data, and as the technology advances to gather more and more information, the amount of data available is predicted to grow exponentially.

We will also get better at analysing these heaps of data, with new tools coming onto the market every week. In fact, Microsoft and Salesforce both recently announced tools to allow non-coders to create apps to view and analyse business data. And as we get better at analysing data, our ability to make predictions improves, too. Market intelligence firm International Data Corporation predicts that half of all business analytics software will include prescriptive analytics abilities by 2020 – which means not only will the software be able to predict customer or user actions, it will be able to make specific recommendations based on those predictions. We're on the cusp of a very exciting time in terms of data and analytics, and the technology available in five or ten years' time could offer possibilities that we can't even imagine yet.

Part of the reason for this explosion in data is the Internet of Things (IoT), sometimes known as the Internet of Everything (IoE). The IoT refers to devices that collect and transmit data via the Internet, and covers everything from your smartphone, smartwatch, Fitbit band, even your TV and refrigerator. The IoT has seen enormous growth in recent years, and it's only just getting started. Today, there are about 13 billion devices that connect to the Internet. By 2020, that number is predicted to rise to anything between 50 and 70 billion. Smartphone users alone are predicted to number over 6 billion by 2020.

Smart devices are transforming our world, our cars, our homes and our businesses. By 2020, a quarter of a billion cars will be connected to the Internet, allowing scope for a whole host of in-vehicle services and automated driving. What was once science fiction is already becoming reality – Google's self-driving cars already clock up several thousand miles a week.

'Wearable' technology is a crucial part of the IoT, and the global market for wearable devices (things like smartphones, Fitbits, etc) grew 223 per cent in 2015. One in six consumers currently owns and uses wearable technology in one way or another. All of these devices create a wealth of data, and we're only just starting to realize the implications of this now.

Connected devices can not only connect to the Internet, they can also connect and share information with each other. In fact, machine-to-machine connections will grow to 27 billion by 2024. So, in the near future, it's not unreasonable to imagine your refrigerator knowing when your milk is out of date and automatically telling your smartphone to order more in the next online shop.

Are we nearing artificial intelligence?

In computing terms, Artificial Intelligence (AI) has been the ultimate goal since the very first computers were invented. It's also been a tantalizing prospect for science fiction writers! But are we finally getting close to realizing AI? Cognitive computing definitely brings us a big step closer.

Combining cognitive science (the study of the human brain) and computer science, cognitive computing looks set to impact almost every area of our lives, from business to healthcare and even our private lives. The aim is to allow a computer to simulate human thought and mimic how our brains work. This allows computers to undertake things that we humans take for granted, like understanding natural language or recognizing objects in a picture.

IBM's Watson system is a prime example of cognitive computing. The system 'learns' as it processes information, so the more data the system is given, the more it learns, and the more accurate it becomes. In practical terms, this technology could be used in any field in which a large amount of complex data needs to be processed and analysed to solve problems, including healthcare, law, education, finance and, of course, business. The technology is already being used in the hospitality industry; Hilton Hotels recently unveiled the first concierge robot, Connie, which can understand natural language and respond to guests' questions about the hotel, local attractions, restaurants, etc.

As computers are more able to think like humans, they enhance our knowledge and capabilities. Just as the heroes of science fiction movies turn to their computers for analysis, predictions and conclusions on what to do next, in real life we're moving into an era where computers can enhance human knowledge in entirely new ways.

Cognitive computing is underpinned by machine learning and deep learning technology, which allows computers to autonomously learn from data. This technology means computers can change and improve their algorithms by themselves, without being explicitly programmed by humans. How does it work? Put simply, if we give the computer a picture of a cat and a picture of a ball, and show it which one is the cat, we can then ask it to decide if subsequent pictures contain cats. The computer compares other images to its training data set (ie the original cat image) and comes up with an answer. Today's machine learning algorithms can do this unsupervised, meaning they do not need their decisions to be pre-programmed. The same principle applies to even more complex tasks, albeit with a much larger training set. Google's voice recognition algorithms, for instance, work from a massive training set, but it's still not nearly big enough to predict every possible word, phrase or question.

But the technology is improving all the time, and machine and deep learning are responsible for advances in computer vision, audio and speech recognition and natural language processing. It is what allows computers to communicate with humans (not always 100 per cent successfully, as Microsoft's slightly crazy, racist Twitter bot proved), and makes Google's self-driving cars possible. It is also the reason Facebook is able to recognize individuals in photos to the same level as humans can, automatically suggesting tags for individuals.

So, is artificial intelligence just around the corner? Probably not, at least not in the science fiction sense. Many scientists believe computers will never be able to 'think' like a human brain. Whichever way you look at it, computers' abilities to see, understand and interact with the world around them are growing at an incredible rate. And as the amount of data we have continues to increase, so too will computers' abilities to learn, understand and react.

The technology has advanced to such an extent that it is now possible for computers to recognize and respond to human emotions. Known as 'affective computing', this technology analyses facial expressions, posture, gesture, tone of voice, speech and even the rhythm and force of keystrokes to register changes in a user's emotional state.

Imagine the potential of this technology. Your computer could recognize when you are frustrated or struggling with a task and provide additional information to help you along. Your phone could tell you to take a break when your stress levels are high. Or, without being asked, your smart home could provide soothing music and lighting when you get in from a bad day at the office. If this all sounds a bit far-fetched, it's not. Leading organizations like Disney, the BBC and Coca-Cola are already partnering with Affectiva, a company specializing in facial recognition technology, to test the effectiveness of adverts and assess how viewers react to content. The same company is also working with a Japanese car company to create in-car technology that can detect when you're distracted or drowsy, and contact emergency services or your next of kin in the event of an emergency. Microsoft has even tested a bra that can sense stress levels in women.

Just as computers can never learn to 'think' in the same way as a human brain, these emotional machines will never really be emotional, but we're nearing the time when machines will at least appear to give us suitable emotional responses. The really exciting part is that we're only just starting to explore the possibilities of all this technology. In 20 years' time, cognitive and affective computing will be mainstream technology.

How data is revolutionizing the world of business

I wholeheartedly believe that big data and its implications will affect every single business – from Fortune 500 enterprises to small businesses – and change how we do business, inside and out. It doesn't matter what field you operate in or the size of your business; as data collection, analysis and interpretation become more readily accessible, they are having an impact on every business.

The key uses of data in business

There are three core areas where data really matters to business: improving decision making, improving operations, and the monetization of data.

First, big data enables companies to collect better market and customer intelligence. With the ever-increasing amount of data available, companies are gaining much better insights into what customers want, what they use (and how), how they purchase goods, and what they think of those goods and services. And this information can be used to make better decisions across all areas of the business, from product and service design to sales and marketing and aftercare.

Second, big data helps companies gain efficiencies and improve their operations. From tracking machine performance to optimizing delivery routes to even recruiting the very best talent, big data can improve internal efficiency and operations for almost any type of business and in many different departments. Companies have even started using sensors to track employee movements, stress, health, and even who they converse with and the tone of voice they use, and using that data to improve employee satisfaction and productivity.

The IoT plays a huge role in improving operational performance. A big part of the IoT isn't so much about smart devices, but about sensors. These tiny innovations can be attached to everything from yogurt cups to the cement in bridges and then record and send data back into the cloud. This will allow businesses to collect more and more specific feedback on how products or equipment are used, when they break, and even what users might want in the future. For example, Rolls-Royce aircraft engines contain sensors that send real-time data on the engine's function back to monitoring stations on the ground. This information can be used to detect malfunctions before they become catastrophic, and possibly to investigate – and hopefully prevent – the causes of aircraft disasters.

Third, data also provides the opportunity for companies to build big data into their product offering – thereby monetizing the data itself. John Deere is an excellent example of a company that is not only using data to benefit its customers, but also as a new product offering. All new John Deere tractors are equipped with sensors that can help the company understand how the equipment is being used, and predict and diagnose breakdowns.

But they've also put the sensors to work for the farmers, offering access to data about when to plant, where, the best patterns for ploughing and reaping, and more. It's become an entirely new revenue stream for what was seen as quite a traditional company.

Let's look at some more examples that demonstrate the wide applicability of big data. For one, supply chain management is a field where big data and analytics have obvious applications. Of course, supply chains have for a long time now been driven by statistics and quantifiable performance indicators. But the sort of analytics that are really revolutionizing industry today – real-time analytics of huge, rapidly growing data sets – were largely absent. Many factors can clearly impact on supply chain management – from the weather to the condition of vehicles and machinery, and so recently leaders in the field have thought long and hard about how this could be harnessed to drive efficiencies.

Applications for data analysis have already been found in inventory management, forecasting, and transportation logistics. In warehouses, digital cameras are routinely used to monitor stock levels and the data provides alerts when restocking is needed. Forecasting takes this a step further – the same camera data can be fed through machine learning algorithms to teach an intelligent stock management system to predict when a resupply will be needed. Opportunities to create efficiency and savings through smart use of data are everywhere and concerted effort is being put into finding them. Eventually, the theory is, warehouses and distribution centres will effectively run themselves with very little need for human interaction.

In retail, both online and offline retailers who are embracing a data-first strategy towards understanding their customers, matching them to products and parting them from their cash are reaping dividends. Today, retailers are constantly finding innovative ways to draw insights from the ever-increasing amount of information available about their customers' behaviour. Big data analytics is now being applied at every stage of the retail process – working out what the popular products will be by predicting trends, forecasting where the demand will be for those products, optimizing pricing for a competitive edge, identifying the customers likely to be interested in them and working out the best way to approach them, taking their money and finally working out what to sell them next.

In banking, The Royal Bank of Scotland (RBS) has developed a big data strategy which it calls 'Personology' in an attempt to reconnect with customers. The bank, which is currently undergoing re-privatization seven years after it was bailed out to the tune of £45 billion by UK taxpayers during the financial crisis, is combining data analytics with a 'back to the

'70s' approach to customer service. The philosophy is one of the developments of the 800-person-strong analytics department, created as part of a £100 million investment in analytic skills and technology across the organization.

The move is about restoring a disconnect which developed between banks and customers after the 1970s. The theory goes that early attempts at data-driven marketing, such as audience segmentation and mass mailing, were too focused on what the banks wanted – usually making sales – and often ignored what customers wanted. The plan is to restore the trust and feeling of support that bank customers would have expected during the 1970s or before – when bank staff would know a customer by name, understand what their needs were on a personal level and attempt to offer services that supported those needs.

As an example of the new strategy in operation, analysts combed financial transaction data to pinpoint situations where customers may have been paying twice for services packaged with bank accounts – such as mobile phone insurance or breakdown assistance. Although at first there were worries that alerting customers to this situation could prompt them to cancel their RBS products in at least some cases, in practice, every single person who was alerted opted to cancel the duplicate third-party service and retain their RBS service.

Other services which fall under the Personology banner include wishing customers a happy birthday if they visit a branch on the day, and automated text messages to let them know that their cash is safe if they accidentally leave it behind after withdrawing it from an ATM.

Big data has even optimized the delivery of your Friday night pizza. Domino's, the world's largest pizza delivery chain, has consistently pushed its brand onto new and developing tech, and it is now possible to order pizzas using Twitter, Facebook, smart watches and TVs, and in-car entertainment systems such as Ford's Synch. So, while it may seem at first glance that pizza and big data are not well matched, the logistics of delivering close to a million pizzas a day across 70 countries throws up exactly the sort of problems that big data is good at overcoming.

Domino's multi-channel approach to interfacing with customers gives them the opportunity to generate and capture a lot of data – which Domino's capitalizes on by using it to improve the efficiency of their marketing. Data captured through all its channels – text message, Twitter, Android, Amazon Echo, to name just a fraction – is fed into the Domino's Information Management Framework. There it's combined with enrichment data from a large number of third-party sources, such as the United States Postal Service, as well as geocode information, and demographic and competitor data, to allow in-depth customer segmentation. This means that individual customers or households can be presented with totally different presentation layers than others – different coupons and product offers – based on statistical modelling of customers fitting their profile. As well as customer segmentation, data is used to assess performance and drive growth at individual stores and franchise groups.

Smart factories and Industry 4.0

First came steam and the early machines that mechanized some of the work our ancestors did. Next came electricity, the assembly line and the birth of mass production. The third era of industry came about with the advent of computers and the beginnings of automation, when robots and machines began to replace human workers on those assembly lines. And now we enter what is being called the fourth industrial revolution, Industry 4.0, in which computers and automation will come together in an entirely new way, with robotics connected remotely to computer systems equipped with machine learning algorithms that can learn and control the robotics with very little input from human operators.

Industry 4.0 introduces the notion of the 'smart factory', in which cyber-physical systems (a combination of computers, networks and physical actions) monitor the physical processes of the factory and make decentralized decisions. In the smart factory, the machines are augmented with web connectivity and connected to a system that can visualize the entire production chain and make decisions on its own. They essentially become IoT systems, communicating and cooperating both with each other and with humans in real time via the wireless web.

For a factory or system to be considered Industry 4.0, it must include the following four features: 1) interoperability, ie machines, devices, sensors and people that connect and communicate with each other; 2) information transparency, where the systems create a virtual copy of the physical world through sensor data in order to contextualize information; 3) technical assistance, both in terms of the ability of the systems to support humans in making decisions and solving problems, and the ability to assist humans with tasks that are too difficult or unsafe for humans; and 4) decentralized decision making, where the cyber-physical systems make simple decisions on their own and become as autonomous as possible.

As with any major shift in industry, there are challenges in adopting this approach. Data security issues are increased when you integrate new systems and increase access to those systems. Systems need to be incredibly reliable and stable for successful cyber-physical operations, and this can be difficult to achieve and maintain, especially when you consider there is a systematic lack of experience and manpower to create and implement these systems. Likewise, avoiding technical problems that could cause expensive production outages is always a concern. In addition, there could be issues with maintaining the integrity and quality of the production process with less human oversight. Finally, whenever new automations are introduced, there is always a risk of losing valuable human jobs. All these issues combined with a general reluctance from stakeholders and investors to invest heavily in costly new technologies means Industry 4.0 has many hurdles to overcome before it becomes mainstream.

But the benefits of an Industry 4.0 model could outweigh the concerns for many production facilities. For example, in very dangerous working environments, the health and safety of human workers could be improved dramatically. Supply chains could be more readily controlled when there is data at every level of the manufacturing and delivery process. Computer control could produce much more reliable and consistent productivity and output. And the results for many businesses could be increased revenues, market share and profits.

In his book *The Fourth Industrial Revolution*,[1] Professor Klaus Schwab, Founder and Executive Chairman of the World Economic Forum, describes how this fourth revolution is fundamentally different from the previous three, which were characterized mainly by advances in technology. In this fourth revolution, we are facing a range of new technologies that combine the physical, digital and biological worlds. These new technologies will impact all disciplines, economies and industries, and even challenge our ideas about what it means to be human. These technologies have great potential to continue to connect billions more people to the web, drastically improve the efficiency of businesses and organizations and help regenerate the natural environment through better asset management, potentially even undoing all the damage previous industrial revolutions have caused.

Reports have also suggested that emerging markets like India could benefit tremendously from Industry 4.0 practices, and the city of Cincinnati, Ohio has declared itself an 'Industry 4.0 demonstration city' to encourage investment and innovation in the manufacturing sector there.

The question, then, is not if Industry 4.0 is coming, but how quickly. I suspect that the early adopters will be rewarded for their courage jumping into this new technology, and those who avoid change risk becoming irrelevant.

Automation and the (very real) threat to jobs

As automation increases, computers and machines will replace workers across a vast spectrum of industries, from drivers to accountants and estate agents to insurance agents. By one estimate, as many as 47 per cent of US jobs are at risk from automation.

When you read or hear news stories about the imminent takeover of robots and algorithms that will eliminate jobs for human workers, many times the first examples given are blue-collar jobs like factory workers and taxi drivers. But plenty of professional jobs may also be at risk of being outsourced to computers. More and more, sophisticated algorithms and machine learning are proving that jobs previously thought to be the sole purview of humans can be done as well or better by machines. Boston Consulting Group has predicted that by 2025, as much as a quarter of jobs currently available will be replaced by either smart software or robots.[2] A University of Oxford study suggested that up to 35 per cent of existing jobs in the UK could be at risk of automation within the next 20 years.[3]

Let's look at some examples. In insurance, formulas have been used for decades to decide how much insurance a person is qualified for and at what rate. But much of what brokers and underwriters do today can be done by computers using big data and machine learning, and new tools are automating this decision-making process even further, reducing the need for human input.

Architects, too, could be under threat. Programs already exist to help individuals design their own homes, making architectural and design choices more automated. For now, these tools are mostly used as visualization tools or to replace architects on very small or simple projects. But as these programs become more sophisticated, the need for human architects and building designers will decrease.

In the financial industry, algorithms can now analyse financial data and prepare accounts (as well as do tax returns) – without the need for accountants. Bank staff have already been partially replaced by ATMs, but soon even higher-level bankers, including loan officers, could be easily replaced by automated systems. Even governments are now using big data and machine learning to check tax returns and identify potential fraud in tax matters. We know that computers are already being used to make stock trades faster than humans ever could and they're even used to predict how the market will react and make recommendations whether you should buy or sell.

Human resources, headhunting and hiring are already being affected by data mining as algorithms take on the job of sorting through resumes to find the perfect candidates. Other traditional human resource tasks, including collecting and filing paperwork, advising employees about benefits, etc, can also be easily automated.

Marketing is all about that most human of skills, persuasion and manipulation. But even that is being successfully outsourced to computers. Persado, a natural language software firm, has put its computers to the task of writing compelling e-mail subject lines for large retail organizations that can as much as double open rates. Companies are also experimenting with automated ad buying – instead of having people choose which magazines to place ads in and on which pages, the computers take care of it, using billions of data points for reference.

Even lawyers, one of the quintessential professions, could be affected. In the discovery phase of a lawsuit, lawyers and paralegals can be required to sift through thousands, even tens of thousands of documents, depending on the case. Now, sophisticated databases can use big data techniques like syntactic analysis and keyword recognition to accomplish the same tasks in much less time. In fact, it's possible that a Watson-style machine learning system could be legally 'trained' to review precedent and case history and even draft legal briefs – traditionally the job of lower-level law firm associates. But don't think it's only the lowly junior associates whose jobs are at risk; lawyers are well paid now to predict the outcome of major cases, but a statistical model created by researchers at Michigan State University and South Texas College of Law was able to predict the outcome of almost 71 per cent of US Supreme Court cases.[4] That ability to predict outcomes is possibly the most valuable (and lucrative) service lawyers provide, and it was easily matched by a computer.

As computers become exponentially more sophisticated, it naturally follows that they will be able to perform more sophisticated work. The obvious downside is that these technological revolutions might not create as many jobs as they eliminate. Certainly, we will need more programmers, statisticians, engineers, data analysts and IT personnel to create and manage these sophisticated computers but not every factory line worker can easily shift gears and become a data analyst.

On the positive side, greater automation will be a boon in many industries, resulting in significantly increased accuracy and productivity. (Any lawyer, for instance, would agree that a faster, more comprehensive discovery phase is a benefit to the legal process.) Ultimately, I believe the possibilities for improving our business decision making, operational processes, products and customer experience are just too big to ignore.

Blockchain technology: the future of data and business?

There's been a lot of hype lately about blockchain technology. In fact, a recent World Economic Forum report predicted that by 2025, 10 per cent of GDP will be stored on blockchains – making it something that every business leader should at least be aware of.[5]

What is blockchain technology? Well, we are used to sharing information through the Internet, but when it comes to transferring value (eg money), we usually revert to centralized financial institutions like banks. Even online payment systems like PayPal generally require a bank account or credit card to use them. Blockchain technology offers the chance to cut out the middle man by carrying out the tasks traditionally handled by financial services organizations, namely recording transactions, establishing identity and establishing contracts. It effectively enables peer-to-peer transactions, much like Bitcoin does (the virtual currency Bitcoin is underpinned by blockchain technology). A blockchain allows anyone to send value anywhere in the world where the blockchain file can be accessed. Each chain is essentially just an online database, stored in a distributed, peer-to-peer fashion among its users. Cryptography ensures that users can only edit the parts of the blockchain that they 'own' – by possessing the private keys necessary to edit the file. By giving private keys which you own to someone else, you effectively transfer the value of whatever is stored in that section of the blockchain.

Microsoft, IBM and many others have announced blockchain-based services, mainly aimed at financial services clients. However, there is vast scope to apply the technology across many other industries – after all, blockchains can be used to store any kind of digital information. The technology could be particularly useful in 'smart contracts', where contracts can be automatically signed off when stated conditions are met. For example, an invoice could be paid automatically when certain conditions are met, or a certain number of orders have been made. And payment could be made automatically using a blockchain payment system.

There's even a theory that blockchain technology could fuel the IoT. For example, devices in the home could automatically pay for the precise energy they use. 'Smart' local power grids could make use of blockchain technology to allow the distribution, metering and billing of electricity to be handled within communities themselves, which would be tremendously useful in remote communities.

I believe blockchain technology could be one of the most powerful data-related developments in the next few years and it's certainly worth business leaders staying abreast of this technology.

Every business must become a data business

It's clear that data is becoming a key business asset, central to the success of every company. As the world becomes smarter and smarter, data becomes the key to competitive advantage, meaning a company's ability to compete will increasingly be driven by how well it can leverage data, apply analytics and implement new technologies. Data and the ability to turn data into business value will become increasingly important in every sector within a few very short years. In fact, according to the International Institute for Analytics, businesses using data will see US $430 billion in productivity benefits over competitors who are not using data by 2020.[6] In business, information is power, and big data is providing information we couldn't have dreamed of collecting or analysing just a few short years ago. Companies that don't evolve and embrace the data revolution will be left behind.

In addition to the growth of companies capturing and using their own data, we will see an explosion of the use of external data (from government sources, external providers, etc). Savvy companies are already predicting this, as with IBM's acquisition of The Weather Channel, mainly for its data.

The International Data Corporation predicts that over the next three to five years, companies will have to commit to digital transformation on a massive scale, including fundamental cultural and operational transformations.[7] Rather than using new technologies to complete old tasks, companies and IT departments will be looking at entirely new functions.

It all starts with a data strategy

In order to thrive, business leaders will have to actively work to expand their thinking away from what has been traditionally done, and include ideas and systems that may never have been considered. Business leaders must begin questioning everything, starting with their strategy. I cannot stress this enough: if every business, regardless of size, is now a data business, every business therefore needs a robust data strategy.

Earlier in the chapter we saw that data matters to businesses in three ways: decision making, operations, and monetization. Your data strategy can cover all three of these areas, or just one, depending on your business. My own recommendation is to look at all three areas in order.

Having a clear data strategy is also critical when you consider the sheer volume of data that is available these days. Those companies who have really profited from the explosion in available data are those who have learned to think smarter about data and what to do with it. Industry-dominating behemoths such as Google, Facebook and Amazon have all been pioneers – not simply collecting vast quantities of data, but finding innovative ways to put it to use. Without a smart plan of action to use the data to produce business insights, the data itself becomes a white elephant – expensive and useless. Therefore, if companies want to avoid drowning in data, they need to develop a smart strategy that focuses on the data they really need to achieve their goals. In other words, this means defining the business-critical questions that need answering and then collecting and analysing only that data which will answer those questions.

I see a lot of companies with data strategies nestled within different areas of the business, such as marketing and sales. That's not enough. Every business needs a company-wide data strategy. Unfortunately, the widespread perception among business executives is that data and analytics are purely IT matters. And as with all IT matters, this means they don't really need to understand how they work, or why. They simply need to know what they do – drive growth – and throw money at them. In my experience, data strategies that are driven by the IT team tend to focus on data storage, ownership and integrity rather than the business's long-term strategic goals and how data can help reach those goals.

Do you need a chief data officer (CDO)?

Larger companies may see the benefit in hiring a CDO who can be responsible for data as a company-wide asset. It seems clear to me that issues of this magnitude – including business opportunities, monetization, data security, privacy, and others – are too big not to be discussed at the C-level, and that therefore any company or organization engaging in serious data projects ought to have a CDO at the top in charge of it all. In fact, recent Gartner statistics show that by 2019, it is expected that 90 per cent of large organizations will have hired a CDO.[8] Ideally, a CDO would have both a technical and business background; too much focus on the technical will result in too much emphasis placed on the tools and bits of data, but too little and the CDO won't be able to effectively communicate with his or her team and the rest of the leadership. Core qualities and requirements of a good CDO include:

- **High-level vision**
  The CDO is responsible for the big picture of the data priorities and strategy for the entire company. To my mind, this means being able to ask the right questions and determine the data and strategies needed to answer those questions. A high level of understanding of both data strategy and the particular business of the organization is required.

- **Implementation**
  The CDO is responsible for the implementation of that strategy at every level within the company. This requires the ability to manage large teams on technical projects and build a business case around technical projects with many variables and uncertainties.

- **Data accuracy, security and privacy**
  The CDO is also the last word on collecting and maintaining accurate data, ensuring data security, and devising and implementing data privacy policies. Because of this, the CDO is the ethical 'conscience' of the company, defining and following ethical guidelines for the collection and use of data.

- **Identifying business opportunities**
  Because of his or her unique relationship to the data, the CDO is the person most responsible for identifying business opportunities discovered through data. In broad terms, the CDO should increase revenue or decrease costs based on the information learned through data initiatives.

- **Data-driven culture leader**
  The CDO must also be the 'charismatic leader' for a data-driven culture within the company. This includes convincing and including everyone from the executive level down to front-line workers of the importance of data, security, and privacy as well as the business value of data.

- **Data as commodity**
  In many cases, the CDO will also be the visionary responsible for recognizing the value in monetizing an organisation's data.

For smaller companies, a CDO may not be necessary or possible, in which case a similar function will be carried out by the leadership team itself, perhaps with the help of an external data consultant. CDO or no CDO, it's clear that data needs to be a top priority for every business. And, as with every major business decision or investment, it all starts with a clear strategy – a roadmap for the journey ahead.

Endnotes

1 Klaus Schwab (2017) *The Fourth Industrial Revolution*, Portfolio Penguin

2 Jane Wakefield (2015) Intelligent machines: the jobs robots will steal first, *BBC*, 14 September, available at: http://www.bbc.com/news/technology-33327659

3 Alan Tovey (2014) Ten million jobs at risk from advancing technology, *The Daily Telegraph*, 10 November, available at: http://www.telegraph.co.uk/finance/newsbysector/industry/11219688/Ten-million-jobs-at-risk-from-advancing-technology.html

4 Kim Ward and Daniel Martin Katz (2014) Using data to predict Supreme Court's decisions, *MSU Today*, 4 November, available at: http://msutoday.msu.edu/news/2014/using-data-to-predict-supreme-courts-decisions/

5 World Economic Forum (2015) Deep shift: technology tipping points and societal impact, available at: http://www3.weforum.org/docs/WEF_GAC15_Technological_Tipping_Points_report_2015.pdf

6 Bloomberg (2016) 6 predictions for big data analytics and cognitive computing in 2016, 6 January, available at: https://www.bloomberg.com/enterprise/blog/6-predictions-for-big-data-analytics-and-cognitive-computing-in-2016/

7 International Data Corporation (2015) IDC predicts the emergence of 'the DX Economy' in a critical period of widespread digital transformation and massive scale up of 3rd platform technologies in every industry, 4 November, available at: https://www.idc.com/getdoc.jsp?containerId=prUS40552015

8 Gartner (2016) Gartner predicts that 90 per cent of large organizations will have a chief data officer by 2019, 26 January, available at: http://www.gartner.com/newsroom/id/3190117

Deciding your strategic data needs 02

Data is certainly exciting – revolutionary, even. But that doesn't always mean useful. To be truly useful, in a business sense, data must address a specific business need, help the organization reach its strategic goals, or generate real value.

I see too many businesses get so caught up in the big data buzz that they collect as much data as possible, without really considering what they want to do with that data. This isn't helpful (and, indeed, as we'll see in Chapter 10, it may land you in legal hot water in the future). Instead of starting with the data itself, it's vital every business starts with strategy. For now, it doesn't matter what data is out there, what data you're already collecting, what data your competitors are collecting, or what new forms of data are becoming available. For now, it doesn't matter whether your business has mountains of analysis-ready data at your disposal, or next to none. A good data strategy is not determined by what data is readily or potentially available – it's about what your business wants to achieve, and how data can help you get there.

The fact is there are many different types of data (as we'll see in Chapter 6). In order to find the right data for you, you must first define how you want to use data. You may need certain types of data for some goals and different types of data for others. Sensor data, for example, is extremely useful for increasing efficiencies in a manufacturing plant, but it's not going to help you predict demand for a new product, or understand how your customers feel about the service you provide.

There are countless ways data can help a business succeed but, broadly speaking, it comes down to the three categories outlined in Chapter 1: using data to improve your decision making, using data to drive operational improvements, and treating data as an asset in itself. In this chapter, I delve deeper into these three categories to help you decide how best to use data in your organization. Chapters 3, 4 and 5 then set out the strategic process for each category.

In practice, even with huge resources, it's tricky to tackle all three categories at the same time. Guiding decision making is certainly the most prevalent way businesses use data today, and broadly speaking, in the majority of organizations, it's usually a good place to start. Therefore, most companies start with decision making and take it from there, building up to operational improvements and, potentially, data as an asset. However, for some companies – large manufacturers for instance – operational improvements may be the top priority. If that's the case in your organization, you can always skip the decision-making aspect for now and revisit it at a later date. And those companies with a mountain of customer data may well be motivated to start treating data as an asset right away. There are no hard and fast rules to making data work for your organization.

Using data to make better business decisions

Making better business decisions is the goal for the majority of clients that I work with and I believe it's something that all businesses should work towards. Whether you want to better understand your market, develop a new product, increase revenue, or target new customers, it all comes down to making better, more informed business decisions. Data provides the insights needed to make those decisions.

Again, it helps to be as specific as possible about what data you want to use and how. In the context of making better decisions, you start by identifying your organization's priorities and unanswered business questions (such as 'how can we target this customer segment?' or 'how can we increase turnover by 10 per cent?'). You then source and analyse the right data to provide insights that help you answer those questions. In this way, having a clear data strategy helps you identify your key business questions and prioritize them, ensuring you use your time and resources in the most effective way. There's more on this in Chapter 3.

You may want to start by focusing on one specific area of the business, such as better understanding your customers, but the underlying idea of making more informed decisions, and building a culture of data-based decision making, should ultimately extend across the whole organization. This is a topic I'm particularly passionate about, and I explore it in more detail in Chapter 11.

Using data to better understand your customers and markets

This is one of the most common (and most publicized) ways companies use data today, and social media in particular has made it easier than ever to build up a rich picture of customers and markets. With a deep understanding of customers and markets, the organization is able to make much smarter decisions – decisions rooted in data, rather than gut feelings or assumptions. There are three key strands to this: getting a full picture of your customers (who they are, where they are, their behaviour, their preferences, etc) so that you can better interact with them; identifying trends; and understanding the competition.

Building a complete picture of your customers can include what makes them tick, why they buy, how they prefer to shop, what they'll buy next, what makes them choose one company over another, and so on. Social media is an obvious and powerful source of this type of information. All of the main social media platforms, including Facebook and Twitter, offer targeted advertising, allowing you to target very precise age groups and geographical areas. Even without spending a penny, social media platforms can be used to see who is talking about what, and determine how that is likely to affect demand for products or services. Twitter – where pretty much all conversations play out in public – is easier to extract insights from than most platforms. In fact, IBM has now partnered with Twitter to offer a service allowing businesses to pull insights directly from tweets. Launching the service back in 2014, IBM gave some powerful examples of the insights that can be gleaned from tweets. These insights included a communications company which was able to reduce customer churn by 5 per cent by predicting where customers were most likely to be affected by loss of service due to bad weather. And a food and drink retailer discovered that high staff turnover was one of the factors which negatively affected the value of their most loyal customers.

Trend spotting is another popular use for data, whether it's industry-wide trends, customer behaviour trends, or indeed any kind of trends that could make a difference to the bottom line. Essentially, this comes down to spotting and monitoring patterns, and using that information to predict where things might go in the future so that you can make better decisions. Marketing is a great example of understanding and predicting trends and, again, social media and the Internet play a large role in this. As individuals, we're used to sharing vast amounts of data about ourselves, our interests, habits, likes and dislikes – whether knowingly or unknowingly – and savvy companies have been quick to capitalize on this information. In addition, trending topics dominate Facebook and Twitter every day, making it easier than ever to determine what people are interested in or what they want.

In retail, online and offline customer behaviour can be measured to microscopic detail. That data can be compared with external data, such as the time of the year, economic conditions and even the weather, to build up a detailed picture of what people are likely to buy, and when. All this information can be used to make smarter decisions on products, promotions, stock levels and communications, to name just a few.

When it comes to understanding your competition, industrial espionage aside, businesses have typically been limited to picking up industry gossip or poking around rivals' websites or stores to glean information. Now, however, data makes it easier than ever to understand what the competition is up to. There is a wealth of data out there on your competitors: financial data is readily available, Google Trends can tell us the popularity of any brand or product, and social media analysis can give valuable insights into a brand or product's popularity (ie how often it is mentioned), and show specifically what customers are saying about that brand or product. Twitter is particularly transparent in this respect. All this information can be compared with your own company or product to guide your decision making. For example, does your competitor get more mentions on Twitter? How do their Twitter conversations with customers compare with yours? Does their Facebook page have more Likes and Shares than yours? Now you can get a much richer picture of your competitors' activities than ever before. The flip side of course is that your competitors will be able to glean just as much information on your performance. But, by routinely gathering useful data and building a culture of data-based decision making, you are well placed to stay one step ahead of the competition.

Seeing data in action – in an unexpected setting

Whether your company is large or small, global or local, high-tech or traditional, data can still help you make better decisions. US restaurant chain Dickey's Barbecue Pit is a prime example of data transforming decision making in an unexpected setting. The firm, which operates more than 500 restaurants across the United States, has developed a proprietary data system called Smoke Stack.

The idea behind Smoke Stack was to get better business insights in order to increase sales, and the ultimate aim was to guide or improve all aspects of Dickey's business decisions, including operations, marketing, training, branding and menu development. The company was already capturing data from a variety of sources, but they did not have the ability to analyse this data in a meaningful, actionable way. They realized they could bring all of that disparate data together in one place, thereby making it easier to use and understand.

Smoke Stack brings together data from point-of-sale systems, marketing promotions, loyalty programmes, customer surveys and inventory systems to provide near-real-time feedback on sales and other key performance indicators. This data is examined every 20 minutes to enable immediate decisions, as well as during a daily morning briefing at corporate HQ, where higher-level strategies can be planned and executed. The near real-time nature of the data is particularly valuable in the restaurant setting, allowing the company to respond 'on the fly' to supply and demand issues. A slow lunchtime and a glut of ribs, for example, can be managed with a simple text message to customers in the local area, inviting them to a ribs special.

Data even plays a part in deciding what goes on the menu. New menu candidates are evaluated by Smoke Stack users according to five metrics – sales, simplicity of preparation, profitability, quality and brand. If the items meet certain targets in all five criteria, they become permanent fixtures on the menu of that particular restaurant.

The restaurant business is extremely competitive and speedy analysis and decision making is a vital part of staying ahead of the competition. As CIO Laura Rea Dickey told me:

> If a region or store is above or below a KPI – whether it is labour or cost of goods – we can deploy resources to course-correct, and we are reacting to those numbers every 12 to 24 hours instead of at the end of every business week or, in some cases, using months-old data. To stay profitable, it is just not reasonable to do business that way anymore.

Data helps Dickey's Barbecue Pit better understand what's occurring on the ground in their restaurants and make quick, informed decisions based on that information. The result is increased sales and a much deeper understanding of customers across different regions.

Using data to improve your operations

This use of data moves away from decision making in favour of optimizing business processes and everyday operations in order to deliver a better product or service. With any business process that generates data (for example, machinery on a production line, sensors on delivery vehicles, customer ordering systems), you can use that data to make improvements and generate efficiencies. In practice, this means putting internal systems in place that allow you to automatically make use of data. The key word there is 'automatically'. Increasingly, this stream is about automating as much as possible.

Transforming your business operations is a big step, bigger than using data to improve decision making, and it's therefore not something that all businesses do. If you feel this area isn't relevant to your organization at this time, that's fine. However, I recommend staying open to operational opportunities.

Gaining internal efficiencies through data

For companies with a manufacturing or industrial focus, machines, vehicles and tools can be made 'smart', meaning they can be connected, data-enabled and constantly reporting their status to each other. Machine data can include anything from IT machines to sensors and meters and GPS devices. Using this data, organizations can gain real-time visibility into their operations. This increases efficiency by allowing every aspect of an industrial operation to be monitored and tweaked for optimal performance. It can also help reduce costly down-time, on the basis that, if we know exactly when to replace a worn part, machinery will break down less often.

This certainly isn't limited to manufacturing businesses. In retail, for example, companies are able to optimize their stock keeping, with stock being automatically replenished when certain conditions are identified or when stock levels drop below a certain number. It is even possible to use predictions generated from social media data, web search trends and weather forecasts to predict demand and top up stock.

As we saw in Chapter 1, supply chain and delivery is another area that can be optimized, thanks to the huge potential of GPS data, traffic data, and even weather data. I know of one pizza delivery company that tracks their drivers using the GPS sensors in their smartphones, giving the company useful insights into how to optimize delivery routes. Essentially, by tracking where their drivers are and monitoring traffic conditions using publicly available data, they're able to deliver to their customers faster and more efficiently.

Big data can also help optimize IT resources. Data and algorithms can be used to identify vulnerabilities in IT systems, reduce risk, detect fraud and monitor cyber security in real time. One example of data-driven fraud detection is credit card companies analysing transactions in real time and shutting down transactions that are suspicious or not possible in real life (such as purchasing something in New York City at 2pm and in New Deli at 3pm using the same card in physical stores). The insurance industry has also made great strides in using data to detect fraud. By analysing the length of time taken to complete a claim online, or by analysing whether a client goes back and changes information on a previous page, they can flag up a potentially fraudulent claim.

Data can even help improve how you recruit and manage your staff – after all, your people are a vital part of your internal operations and processes. Sometimes, finding and keeping the right people can be the key to maintaining a competitive edge. Data can help you find the very best candidates, understand whether your current recruitment channels are effective, and help keep your existing employees happy. For example, one client of mine wanted to recruit self-driven people that were able to use their own initiative. By analysing different data sets from the type of people they wanted to recruit and those they wanted to avoid, the company found that candidates who filled out applications with browsers that were not pre-installed on their computers and instead had to be installed separately (such as Firefox or Chrome) tended to be better for that particular job. Measuring this simple indicator allowed the company to eliminate those that didn't meet the criteria before interview stage, thereby finding the right sort of people more easily. Another one of my clients, a retailer, analyses the social media profiles of candidates to (very accurately!) predict the level of intelligence and emotional stability of potential candidates.

The operational applications go way beyond recruitment. HR data, such as absenteeism figures, productivity data, personal development reviews, and staff satisfaction data, can all be analysed for insights. In addition to these somewhat traditional types of HR data, data can be captured in many new and exciting ways, such as capturing employees on CCTV, scanning social media data, analysing the content of e-mails, and even monitoring where staff are by using the data from geo-positioning sensors in corporate smartphones. Once again, the challenge is to establish which data is really going to make an impact on your company's performance, to avoid getting caught up in the overwhelming array of possibilities. You need to consider what is most useful from an operational perspective. It might, for example, be increasing employee satisfaction in order to reduce staff turnover. Plus, to avoid any sort of backlash, it's very important that staff are made aware of precisely what data is being gathered from them, and what it is being used for. Everyone needs to be aware that the purpose is to increase overall company efficiency, rather than assess or monitor individual members of staff in a Big Brother-type fashion.

Amazon, and how data optimizes business processes to increase sales

We all know that Amazon pioneered e-commerce in many ways, but possibly one of its greatest innovations was the personalized recommendation system – which, of course, is built on the big data it gathers from its millions of customer transactions. Psychologists speak about the power of suggestion – put something that someone might like in front of them and they may well be overcome by a burning desire to buy it, regardless of whether or not it will fulfil any real need. This is of course how impulse advertising has always worked. However, instead of a scattergun approach, Amazon leveraged their customer data and honed its system into a high-powered, laser-sighted sniper rifle. Their systems are getting better all the time, and it looks like what we have seen so far is only the beginning. In a much-publicized move, Amazon has now obtained a patent on a system designed to ship goods to us before we have even decided to buy them – predictive despatch. This is a strong indicator that their confidence in reliable predictive analytics is increasing.

Amazon has also incorporated big data analysis into its customer service operations. Its purchase of shoe retailer Zappos is often cited as a key element in this. Since its founding, Zappos had earned a fantastic reputation for its customer service and was often held up as a world leader in this respect. Much of this was due to their sophisticated relationship management systems which made extensive use of their own customer data. These procedures were melded together with Amazon's own, following the 2009 acquisition.

Amazon has grown far beyond its original inception as an online bookshop, and much of this is due to its enthusiastic adoption of big data principles and using data to improve the way it operates.

Uber, and how data is transforming transport

Uber is a smartphone app-based taxi booking service which connects users who need to get somewhere with drivers willing to give them a ride. The business is rooted firmly in data, and leveraging data in a more effective way than traditional taxi firms has played a huge part in its success.

Uber's entire business model is based on the very big data principle of crowd sourcing; anyone with a car who is willing to help someone get to where they want to go can offer to help get them there. Uber stores and monitors data on every journey its users take, and uses it to determine demand, allocate resources and set fares. The company also carries out in-depth analysis of public transport networks in the cities it serves, so it can focus coverage in poorly served areas and provide links to buses and trains.

Uber holds a vast database of drivers in all of the cities it covers, so when a passenger asks for a ride, they can instantly match you with the most suitable drivers. In a crucial difference from regular taxi services, customers are charged for the time the journey takes, not the distance covered. The company has developed algorithms to monitor traffic conditions and journey times in real time, meaning prices can be adjusted as demand for rides changes, and traffic conditions mean journeys are likely to take longer. This encourages more drivers to get behind the wheel when they are needed – and stay at home when demand is low. The company has applied for a patent on this method of data-based pricing, which it calls 'surge pricing'. It is an advanced form of 'dynamic pricing', if you like – similar to that used by hotel chains and airlines to adjust price to meet demand – although rather than simply increasing prices at weekends or during public holidays, Uber uses predictive modelling to estimate demand in real time.

Uber works with many different types of data. For example, it calculates fares automatically using GPS, traffic data and the company's own algorithms which make adjustments based on the time that the journey is likely to take. The company also analyses external data such as public transport routes to plan services.

Uber is not alone in using data to revolutionize transport. It has competitors offering similar services on a (so far) smaller scale, such as Lyft, Sidecar and Haxi. Ultimately, the most successful company is likely to be the one that best uses data to improve the service it provides to customers.

Rolls-Royce, and how data drives manufacturing success

Rolls-Royce manufactures enormous engines which are used by 500 airlines and around 150 armed forces. In a high-tech industry like this, failures and mistakes can cost billions – not to mention human lives. It's therefore crucial the company is able to monitor the health of its products to spot potential problems before they occur. With this in mind, Rolls-Royce uses data in three key areas of its operations: design, manufacture, and after-sales support.

In design terms, data is used in product simulations to model and predict how components and engines will perform under certain circumstances. As the company's chief scientific officer, Paul Stein, told me:

> We have huge clusters of high-power computing which are used in the design process. We generate tens of terabytes of data on each simulation of one of our jet engines. We then have to use some pretty sophisticated computer techniques to look into that massive data set and visualize whether that particular product we've designed is good or bad.

In fact, they eventually hope to be able to visualize their products in operation in all the potential extremes of behaviour in which they get used, and they are already working towards this.

The company's manufacturing systems are increasingly becoming networked and communicating with each other in the drive towards a networked, Internet of Things industrial environment. The company generates a huge amount of data in its own manufacturing processes. For example, at their new factory in Singapore, Rolls-Royce is generating half a terabyte of manufacturing data on each individual fan blade. As they produce 6,000 fan blades a year at that plant, that's a lot of data being generated from just one component. This data is useful in many ways, not least to monitor quality control of the components manufactured.

In terms of after-sales support, Rolls-Royce engines and propulsion systems are all fitted with hundreds of sensors which record every tiny detail about their operation and report any changes in real time to engineers on the ground. The company uses this data to identify factors and conditions under which engines might need maintenance. In some situations, humans manually intervene to avoid or mitigate against whatever is likely to cause a problem, but, increasingly, Rolls-Royce expects that computers will carry out the intervention themselves.

With civil aero engines as reliable as they are, the emphasis shifts to keeping them performing at their best, thereby saving airlines fuel and ensuring they meet their schedules. Using data, Rolls-Royce can identify maintenance actions days or weeks ahead of time, so airlines can schedule the work without passengers experiencing any disruption. To support this, analytics on board the engines crunch through large volumes of data generated during each flight, and transmit the pertinent highlights to ground for further analysis. Once at the gate, the whole flight data is available for engineers to examine and detect the fine margins of performance improvement. Engineers look for anomalies in the data, such as in pressure, temperature and vibration measurements, to identify when an engine needs to be serviced. And, in the event that something goes wrong, having all this data to hand means the company is able to identify everything which contributed to the problem. They use this information to predict when and where the problem is likely to repeat itself, and this information then feeds back into the design process – bringing the process full circle.

Rolls-Royce serves as a great example of a traditional manufacturing company transitioning to the new age of data-enabled improvement and efficiency. Ultimately, data and analytics has helped Rolls-Royce stream-line its product design, decrease product development time and improve the quality and performance of its products. And, although it doesn't give precise figures, the company says that adopting this data-driven approach has 'significantly' reduced costs. As Stein puts it, 'The digitization of Rolls-Royce is not up for debate; the question is not whether it will happen but how fast it will happen.'

Transforming your business model: data as a business asset

As well as helping you make better decisions and improve your operations, data can even become a key part of your business model. There are two streams to this: one is data becoming a very valuable asset that increases the overall value of the company, the other is about the ability to monetize data by selling it back to customers or other interested parties.

How data can boost the value of your company

Companies are now being bought and sold based on the data they have. In 2015, IBM announced it was acquiring most of The Weather Company, which owns Weather.com and Weather Underground, for a reported US $2 billion. Why? For the company's data. Its weather-related data sets are vast, including data from 3 billion weather forecast reference points, 50,000 flights and more than 40 million smartphones per day. It's no wonder then that nearly three-quarters of The Weather Company's scientists work in data and computers (as opposed to the one-quarter who are atmospheric scientists and meteorologists). Now IBM has access to all that data and can sell it to other companies who need to know about the weather. Reliable weather data is increasingly important in many, many industries, way beyond the obvious ones like agriculture and transportation. Weather patterns affect retail shopping, for example. And large weather events can have a lasting impact on everything from construction to the insurance industry. Pharma companies even use weather data to predict demand for flu and cold medicines. As Doug Laney, analyst at leading IT research company Gartner, tweeted, '60 per cent of S&P blame their earnings miss on the weather.' Because of all this, a company that can accurately predict weather patterns becomes a very savvy investment indeed.

In another example, Microsoft recently announced that it was purchasing LinkedIn for US $26.2 billion, giving Microsoft access to the professional network's more than 400 million users – and the data they generate. Microsoft has said that, while LinkedIn will function as a semi-autonomous entity, its data will be integrated with Microsoft's collaboration and productivity tools. This potentially allows great scope for personalization within Microsoft's tools, and could help them become more competitive in the enterprise market against big competitors like Google Apps for Work.

As we can see, the basic principle here is that data in itself is an asset. Indeed, Gartner has coined the term 'infonomics' to cover the increasing value of information in its own right. As data becomes a core asset, however, the need for careful data governance becomes even more pressing. Echoing this, a recent Gartner Research Circle study found the biggest concern around data was 'governance and privacy'.[1] I talk more about data security and governance in Chapter 10.

Turning your data into a new revenue stream

Let's explore the other aspect of monetizing data: selling access to your data. If your company is generating or gathering data, it is worth considering whether there is a secondary market for that data. In other words, can you sell that data back to customers? Or can you sell it elsewhere, perhaps in a different format?

Fitbit is a prime example of a product manufacturer that is now a data merchant. Based on the notion that informed people make smarter lifestyle choices, Fitbit's devices encourage people to eat well and exercise more by helping them monitor and improve their habits. Fitbit tracks the user's activity, exercise, calorie intake, and sleep. Clearly health data like this is incredibly informative and valuable, beyond even the individual user. As such, Fitbit aggregates data about fitness habits and health stats to share with strategic partners. Personal, individual data can also be shared, with the user's permission. Microsoft's HealthVault service, for instance, allows users to upload and share data from their fitness tracker with health professionals, potentially giving doctors a more complete picture of a patient's overall health and habits than could be gained just through consultations and examinations. And the implications go even further, with the recent announcement that insurance company John Hancock is offering a discount to policyholders who wear a Fitbit device. Policyholders can share their Fitbit data in return for rewards linked to their physical activity and diet. This indicates an increasing willingness among individuals to 'trade' their private data in return for an improved product/service or financial reward – all of which is great, so long as the transaction is transparent, ie the individual is aware of exactly what data they're giving up and why. Fitbit is also now selling its trackers and special tracking software to employers such as BP America so that they can track their employees' health and activity levels (with their permission). In fact, this is one of the Fitbit's fastest-growing business areas.

Facebook provides another simple example of this process in action. The social network is free to users, but has historically generated income from advertising. Now, the company is capitalizing on the huge amount of data it has on its users by making certain user data available to other businesses – for a fee. Amazon, too, has commercialized its data on an impressive scale. And, unlike Facebook, Amazon's data relates to how we spend cold, hard cash – which makes it especially valuable to businesses. So, having worked out how to use its data to get more money out of our pockets, Amazon is now helping other businesses do the same, by making that data, as well as its own tools for analysing it, available to buy. This means that, as with Google, we have started to see adverts driven by Amazon's platform and based on its data appearing on other sites over the past few years. As noted by *MIT Technology Review*, this makes the company now a head-on competitor to Google – with both online giants fighting for a chunk of marketers' budgets.[2]

Even if you aren't a big data giant like Facebook or Amazon, even if you aren't generating data on a 'big' scale like Fitbit, data could still become a key business asset. In short, if you have the ability to generate data, you may find that data could prove valuable above and beyond what it was originally intended for.

The importance of the *right* data, not *all* data

However you plan to use data, even if you plan to treat data as a key business asset, it is never a good idea to capture huge mountains of data that you don't really need. Remember, the power of big data is not in the data itself, it's in how you use it. I've long argued that simply collecting data or even analysing it isn't the end game of a data strategy. Instead, it's about how you use the information you glean from the data. It's about the processes you improve, the better decisions you're able to make, the business value you add. Data for data's sake is meaningless. Therefore, instead of hoarding data, collect only what you really need and what makes business sense.

Sure, the real big data giants like Google never throw data away. Every tiny piece of data may be valuable. Everything is captured and analysed because it can potentially offer unique and powerful insights for business development. Even errors are captured and analysed. You might think, for example, that misspelled words and errors in search queries could be discarded, but you'd be wrong. Google captures that data and uses it to create the world's best spell checker. Remember though that giants like Google and Amazon have the expertise, money and technology to cope with massive data sets. They have the storage capacity, manpower, analytical know-how and software to mine all that data for insights. Most companies, even large organizations, will never be in that position. Nor should they be. I believe the need to stay focused is a good thing.

Rather than trying to collect as much data as possible, it is far better to collect only the data that you really need to meet your goals. Creating a thorough data strategy will help you do this, but it's also important to keep revisiting that strategy in order to stay lean and remain focused on the outcomes.

But what if you want to treat data as an asset or create a new revenue stream by selling data? Isn't it a good idea to gather as much of it as possible? Actually, no. Even when treating data as an asset, you still need a very clear idea of what type of data you want to collect, and who you might sell that data to, to ensure you collect the most valuable data.

We need only look at the backlash against streaming music service Spotify to understand why it's never a good idea to collect data for data's sake. In 2015, the company released a new privacy policy. Among the new terms, Spotify claimed the right to go through your phone and access your photos, media files, GPS location, sensor data (like how fast you're walking), and your contacts. The terms would also allow Spotify to share this data with advertisers, music rights holders, mobile networks, and other 'business partners'. Of course, the free version of the service is supported by ad revenue, but these terms also applied to the platform's 30 million paying users. The reaction from users was swift and negative. A huge outcry erupted on Twitter and other social networking sites, with users saying they would leave the service rather than agree to the new terms.

Part of the problem stemmed from the fact that the new privacy policy was extremely vague about exactly what data was being collected, when, why, and with whom it was shared. The huge backlash against this lack of transparency prompted the company's CEO, Daniel Ek, to issue an apology and clarify the company's position and intentions.[3] This included the promise that 'We will ask for your express permission before accessing any of this data – and we will only use it for specific purposes that will allow you to customize your Spotify experience'.

Making a strong business case for data

As well as deciding how you want to use data, an important part of creating a robust data strategy is making a strong business case for using data in your organization – a business plan of sorts – and communicating the key elements of the plan across the organization. I think this is an essential part of getting people on board with using data. If your people are aware of and excited by the possibilities of data, they are far more likely to buy into the idea.

When making a case for big data, there are certain details that cannot be overlooked. These include an outline of the data strategy and its goals, ie what the organization is hoping to find out or achieve with data. In addition, you should set out the tangible benefits to the business, ie how data will help you improve or transform your business. It is also important to be clear on the capabilities needed and any potential skills gaps in the organization, plus how you to intend to fill these gaps (there's more on data capabilities and skills in Chapter 9). Finally, it's vital to be open and realistic about the timeframe, likely disruption to the business, and costs. To ensure you have a truly robust business case for data, it's important not to gloss over these issues – after all, working with data can be expensive (not always, but often), and implementing operational changes can be disruptive.

When you have built a solid argument for using big data in your business, you should promote and evangelize it across the whole company. How you communicate your data plan across the company depends on a number of factors, such as the size of your company and your usual processes for kicking off new initiatives. Not everyone in the company will need to know the ins and outs of big data analysis and costs, but distilling the plan down into the key nuggets is a good way to get buy-in across the company.

I can't stress enough how important this stage is; 'selling' big data to your people is a crucial early step on your data journey. It instils confidence in data. This is especially critical if you are using data to improve your decision making across the company. When your people understand the value of data to the organization, they are much more likely to incorporate it into their decisions in future. However, you plan to use data, you want everyone in the organization to be in love with the general idea of using data. For more on fostering a data culture across the organization, turn to Chapter 11.

Endnotes

1 Cath Everett (2015) British breakthrough for IoT-based business applications this year, *Computer Weekly*, available at: http://www.computerweekly.com/ feature/British-breakthrough-for-IoT-based-business-applications-this-year

2 Tom Simonite (2016) Google and Microsoft want every company to scrutinize you with AI, *MIT Technology Review*, 1 August, available at: https://www. technologyreview.com/s/602037/google-and-microsoft-want-every-company-to-scrutinize-you-with-ai/

3 Spotify CEO Daniel Ek issued this apology: https://news.spotify.com/us/2015/ 08/21/sorry-2

Using data 03
to improve your
business decisions

Data is becoming an increasingly important input into the decision-making process, and improving decision making is probably the most widespread way businesses are using data today. This is a broad category, covering any way in which data can help people in the organizations make better decisions. 'People' is the crucial word there. The data user, if you like, in this scenario is a human being. We are not talking about machines automatically carrying out an action based on what the data tells them (such as Amazon's product recommendations, which are generated automatically based on data and algorithms). This chapter refers exclusively to the process of human beings in an organization interpreting data in order to make smarter, more informed decisions. Smarter decisions being, essentially, anything that moves the organization closer to achieving its strategic goals.

I feel data should be at the heart of decision making in all businesses, regardless of their size or industry sector. Of course, experience and instinct play a role in good decision making, but they are not enough in today's competitive business world. Data provides the extra edge that businesses will need to succeed going forward. Data provides valuable insights that help you answer critical business questions like 'How satisfied are our customers?' And those insights can be turned into decisions and actions that improve the business.

Setting out your key business questions

You can't identify what data you need if you aren't clear about what it is you want to find out. Having very clear objectives in mind helps you get the most out of data. That's why the process of data-based decision making always starts in the same place: identifying your key business questions.

Your key business questions (or strategic questions, if you prefer) are those unanswered questions that relate to core areas of your business and its goals. In other words, *what do you need to know to be able to achieve your strategic goals?* Focusing on key questions helps you hone in on the data you really need – because once you know the questions you need to answer, it's much easier to identify the data that will help you answer those questions.

I recommend looking at four key areas of your organization to identify your objectives and key business questions. Those areas are: 1) customers, markets and competition; 2) finance; 3) internal operations; and 4) people. I look at each of these areas in turn below. You may choose to look at all four areas at once, or you may need to focus only on one specific area (say, if an area is underperforming). Either way, the process is the same. First you set out your strategic objectives for that business area (ie what you are trying to achieve), then you identify the questions that relate to those objectives (ie what you need to know if you are to meet those goals). If you already have a comprehensive strategic plan in place, you can simply identify the questions that tie in with your corporate objectives. For example, if your objective is to increase your customer base, your key business questions might include, 'Who are currently our customers?', 'What are the demographics of our most valuable customers?' and 'What is the lifetime value of our customers?'

Once you have created your list of questions, you may need to spend some time prioritizing and narrowing the list down. A list of 100 questions, for instance, is too long to be workable. I suggest that, if you are looking at all four business areas, try to narrow it down to your top 10 questions per area (if your list is smaller than 10 questions, even better). In other words, if you could only answer a handful of questions, which would you choose? Focus on the key questions that are most important to achieving your overall strategy. Any leftover questions can always be answered further down the line.

If you are focusing on one particular business area you can perhaps extend the list to 25 questions if you need to. However, if focusing on just one area, be aware of potential impact on other core areas of the business. For example, if you focus only on customer-related questions, you will need to consider the financial, operational and people-related implications of any decisions.

Good questions lead to better answers

In Douglas Adams' *The Hitchhiker's Guide to the Galaxy*, a race of creatures build a supercomputer to calculate the meaning of 'life, the universe, and everything'. After hundreds of years of processing, the computer announces that the answer is '42'. When the beings protest, the computer calmly suggests that now they have the answer, they need to know what the actual question is – a task that requires a much bigger and more sophisticated computer.

This is why it's so important to start with the right questions. When you start with a simple question and then gather only the data that can directly answer that question, data suddenly becomes much more manageable. You no longer need to be concerned with all possible sources of data, and all the new and interesting types of data that are becoming available. You need only focus on the data that will help with the task at hand. In this way, the right business questions are very powerful things. The right business questions help you get to the heart of what's important and what's not. The right business questions help you identify your company's biggest concerns. They guide discussion. And, most importantly, they help people make better decisions.

Here's an example showing the power of clear business questions. I once worked with a small fashion retail company that had no data other than their traditional sales data. They wanted to increase sales but had no data to draw on to help them achieve that goal. Together we worked out that the specific questions they needed to answer included:

- How many people actually pass our shops?
- How many stop to look in the window and for how long?
- How many of them then come into the shop?
- How many then buy?

To answer these questions, first we installed a small, discreet device into the shop windows that tracked mobile phone signals, counting everyone who walked past the shops (or rather, everyone with a mobile phone on them, which, these days, is almost everyone) – thereby answering the first question. The sensors also measured how many people stopped to look at the window and for how long, and how many people then walked into the store – answering the second and third questions. And we used ordinary sales data to record how many people actually bought something. By combining the data from the sensors placed in the window with transaction data, we were able to measure conversion ratio and test window displays and various offers to see which ones increased the conversion rate. Not only did the retailer increase sales by understanding what drew customers to stop and come into their stores, but they also used the insights to make a significant saving by closing one of their stores. The sensors were able to finally tell them that the footfall reported by the market research company prior to opening in that location was wrong and the passing traffic was insufficient to justify keeping the store open.

Questions related to your customers, markets and competition

Closely aligned with the organization's sales and marketing function, this is about identifying the questions that help you build a comprehensive picture of your customers, markets and competitors. As such, you need to consider how much you currently know about the customers your strategy is targeting (including customer behaviours, patterns and segmentation) and the market within which you operate. You should also consider what competition you will be up against as you work towards realizing your strategic goals and what risks you may face. Key business questions in this area may include:

- What are some of the key trends in our market?
- Is there any upward or downward trend in demand for our product or service offerings?
- Will there still be demand for our product over the next five years?
- Which markets should we abandon, and when?
- Why are some customers not buying from us?
- How are customer buying patterns and customer expectations shifting?
- How do we best segment our customers?
- Who are our key competitors going to be and why?
- How do we best price our products or services?
- What marketing or sales channels are most effective?
- How does our brand compare with those of our competitors?
- How satisfied are our customers with our service?
- What is the average length and value of a customer relationship?
- How well are our customers engaging with us on social media?
- What are the key customer churn trends?

For example, it is likely that you will reach different segments of your market via different channels, but is it still important to know which channels are working and which ones are less effective so you can make better marketing decisions. There are many possible channels and ways to market your products and services, from traditional print ads, PR, media and direct marketing to guerrilla marketing, online marketing and social media. Understanding which delivers most bang for your buck is essential. (This is where the old marketing adage comes from: 50 per cent of all marketing spend is wasted but the problem is we don't know which 50 per cent!) Marketing channel analytics looks at costs and return on investment so that the marketing budget can be used more effectively. It can help you answer business questions like 'What type of marketing is more cost effective for reaching our customers?', 'What marketing channel is most effective?', or 'Is online marketing more effective for us than offline marketing?'

Say your marketing channel analytics show that your most effective method of marketing is direct marketing, yielding consistently high response rates and a very good return on investment. Your online promotions come in second place. However, when you take costs into consideration, the online promotions are a clear winner because, although they don't yield quite as much income, they are significantly cheaper to implement. The sensible business decision, therefore, is to invest in more online promotions. This may not have been apparent without data and analytics, and the company would have continued spending more than it needed to on costly direct marketing promotions.

Let's look at a couple of real-life examples of how data can provide useful insights about customers, markets and sales. US telecommunications company Sprint has access to vast amounts of user data, thanks to its huge network of users. Three years ago, it formed a subsidiary, Pinsight Media, to help capitalize on that data and inform advertising decisions. Jason Delker, chief technology and data officer at Pinsight, explained to me that mobile network data is uniquely valuable, because it can be directly linked to a real bill-paying customer. Much of the digital information generated online is linked to nothing more substantial than an e-mail address, which can easily be set up with limited or even false information. Mobile network user data, however, is far more likely to be tied to a real person (their credentials having been checked through credit records, etc, when they opened their account).

Take GPS locational data, for example. If you use an Android or iPhone, app developers (with your permission) can see where you are, and use data about your geographical location and daily routine to provide you with relevant services or advertising. However, they aren't tracking you as such. All they are tracking is an e-mail address, which could have been set up using fake details or shared between different devices or users. In contrast, Pinsight correlates locational data with verified demographic data acquired from the billing process. 'As a result', explained Delker, 'we have a better insight into what types of ads we may be able to place based on the information we have about a specific subscriber'. Interestingly, they have found that self-reported data is often substantially different from Pinsight's data, which has been authenticated using network data. This indicates that ads based on self-reporting data may not be very relevant to the user.

As well as locational data, Pinsight also uses its network technology and infrastructure to authenticate demographic and customer behaviour data. For example, the company can monitor what services, such as Facebook or Twitter, are being used on devices, and for how long (the contents, ie how that service is being used, remain encrypted). This helps them understand more about user behaviour.

Obviously, with access to such detailed and intimate personal data, privacy is very important. With this in mind, Sprint and Pinsight decided to make everything dependent on the user opting in. As Delker put it:

> One of the most important things to us is essentially opt-out and opt-in data – Sprint is the only one of the four large wireless US operators that by default opts everyone out. What I mean by that is that we basically say we won't use a subscriber's behavioural data to target ads at them without permission. We try to convince them – and it's been very easy to do – that if they actually let us leverage that data, we will send them things that are more relevant and so ads become less of a nuisance and more of a service – consumers are pretty wise to the fact that those types of services help fund and lower the cost of an operator's core mobile services.

In this way, Sprint and Pinsight show us that it's possible to gather a wealth of data without trying to trick the user into giving up personal data. This is an important point, and I talk more about transparency and privacy in Chapter 10. For now, the takeaway point is that if you are upfront about how you intend to use the data, and what the user gets in return, ultimately you end up with more useful (and therefore valuable) data as a result. And the value to Sprint is significant. In the three years since Pinsight was established, the company has gone from serving zero to six billion ad impressions per month.

Another interesting example of using data to inform decisions comes from an unlikely source: Wimbledon 2016. Organizers have invested in advanced analytics in order to capture tennis fans' attention on social media and online platforms. A big event like Wimbledon generates hundreds of thousands of social media and online posts. Using IBM's Watson analytics platform, it's now possible to crunch through all that data to find the stories that fans are most engaged with, understand the sort of content they most want to see, and then use that information to drive content creation. Interestingly, rather than piggybacking on trends once they occur, Watson can spot emerging trends – such as an unexpectedly good performance by players from a particular nation – before they start to trend on Twitter.

Why is this useful? In 2014, three Canadian players – Milos Raonic, Eugenie Bouchard and Vasek Pospisil – all reached the semi-finals of major tournaments. This generated a lot of unexpected conversation about Canadian tennis and where this (seemingly overnight) success had come from. Broadcasters and media had to engage with this topic reactively. By pre-empting a trending topic like this, media teams could have adapted their content to explain why the Canadians were doing so well all of a sudden. As Alexandra Willis, head of communications, content and digital at the All England Lawn Tennis and Croquet Club, which hosts the yearly grand slam, puts it, 'We will hopefully be able to monitor the particular interest in a particular court, or if there is one player garnering particular interest we will be able to hop on and pre-empt that trend.' Using this information, the content team will create relevant social media posts, alerts and reports. Thus, the data provides insights that help drive editorial decisions.

You may wonder why social media posts are relevant to a seemingly traditional tennis tournament that is primarily watched through the TV. At the time of writing, the TV audience stands at around 300 million while the audience across all digital platforms tops out at around 30 million. Wimbledon is investing in the small portion of fans who engage with tennis through digital means because that figure is very likely to grow in future. They're therefore making sure they can serve (no pun intended) different customer segments in the most appropriate way. As Willis explains:

> There is a very important audience who like to sit and watch tennis on TV for hours on end, but there's also an audience who like to receive personalized alerts during a match, or while they are at work, and an audience that likes to sit on their Facebook page and watch content as it is served to them. Our challenge is making sure that we are servicing each of those audiences on all of those platforms in the best way we can, while making sure that we are being true to Wimbledon's tone of voice and what our purpose is.

In this way, data helps Wimbledon plan for the future and maintain relevance in a crowded sports media environment.

Questions related to finance

The aim here is to consider how much you currently know about the financial implications of your strategy, and what unanswered questions you have. It is about identifying and predicting key financial indicators like revenue, cashflow and share price performance – specifically identifying the things you know for sure, and those that are based on guesswork or assumptions. Armed with your unanswered financial questions, you can use data to deliver greater certainty and, therefore, more informed decisions.

Your key finance questions may include:

- How does our strategy generate money?
- What assumptions have we made about revenue, profit and growth as we implement our strategic plan?
- What are our key sales, revenue and profit trends?
- Who are our most and least profitable customers?
- What are our most and least profitable products or services?
- What does our cash conversion cycle look like?
- How much will it cost to produce and deliver our products/services over the next 12 months?
- What is our share price likely to be over the next 12 months?
- Where are our biggest cost-saving opportunities?

For example, say you wanted to explore your most (and least) profitable customers. There is often an assumption in business that any customer is a good customer but that's not always the case. Customer profitability usually falls within the Pareto principle, or 80/20 rule, whereby 20 per cent of your customers are likely to account for 80 per cent of your profit. Conversely, there is also likely to be another 20 per cent of your customers that account for 80 per cent of your customer-related costs. Knowing which is which is important. If you can't differentiate between the customers that make you money and the customers that lose you money then you will treat all your customers the same and diminish your profitability.

When you can split your customers into groups, you can tailor your marketing message and your level of service to each group. Customer profitability analytics provide you with a deep understanding of your customers' buying habits and the costs incurred in supplying the products they buy from you. Armed with this knowledge, you can focus on the highest profit centres by really looking after those customers that are profitable (and perhaps encouraging the ones that cost you money to go to your competition).

By understanding the profitability of certain groups of customers, you can also analyse each group to look for any similarities within them, such as where they live, what they first purchased or where they were sourced from. You might, for example, discover that your most profitable customers made their first purchase from a particular advertisement in a particular magazine. Insights like that can help direct your future marketing efforts to attract more profitable customers. Therefore, customer profitability analytics can help you answer more than the simple question of who are the most and least profitable customers; it can also help you answer questions like 'How do our marketing initiatives stack up against each other?' and 'How do various sales people and regions compare?'

Say you provide electronic parts to large manufacturers. You may have 10,000 customers on your database going back many years. By using customer profitability analytics, you can divide those 10,000 customers into percentage groups from the top 10 per cent to the bottom 10 per cent, based on a variety of identifiers, such as product, region, volume of sales, frequency of sales, and customer service issues. You may discover, for example, that one particular customer that your sales team love (and spend a lot of time on) because they buy so frequently is actually a loss-making client, based on the level of after-sales support they require. So, while this customer looks good on paper, they waste a huge amount of time questioning and complaining about aspects of the product or delivery that renders them unprofitable. Knowing this, you can direct your sales team to focus on more profitable customers.

Even not-for-profit organizations can benefit from profitability analytics. They may not have 'customers' as such, but not-for-profits do have 'users'. In addition, such organizations certainly need to manage costs carefully and make their budgets stretch as far as possible. For example, I once did some work with the National Health Service in the UK. Using customer profitability analytics, we discovered that just 5 per cent of their patients were responsible for over 200 visits to the accident and emergency department. They were 'super-users', if you like, who clearly had issues beyond the immediate reason they were presenting in A&E. By pinpointing these super-users, staff were able to seek special assistance for them, thereby freeing up valuable resources for other users.

In another example, Caesars Entertainment used data analytics to understand customer profiles and how money was being spent in their resorts. The company runs hotels and casinos around the world, including some of the most famous casinos in Las Vegas. They hit turbulent times recently, with parts of the operation facing bankruptcy, and have been hit with a US $1.5 million fine over irregularities in their accounts. During these proceedings, though, it emerged that the individual asset most highly prized by the company – above even their property portfolio – was their customer database, containing data on 45 million hotel and casino customers around the world.

Caesars (formerly known as Harrah's) invested heavily in big data and analytics to allow them to gain an in-depth understanding of their customers and, of course, encourage them to carry on spending money. The US casino industry has been in decline for many years, in terms of money spent at the gaming tables. Casino operators have therefore had to look elsewhere to increase their incomes – namely, drinks, food and entertainment.

With this in mind, the Caesars Total Rewards scheme is used to gather data on customers' behaviour as they move around the facilities and partake in the various entertainments and refreshments. Social media data is also captured, and players are incentivized to link their Facebook accounts to their Total Rewards accounts, 'check in' on social networks, and post pictures taken at resorts. Thanks to this in-depth customer data, the company went from being able to trace the journey of 58 per cent of the money spent in their casinos to 85 per cent. One key finding was that the vast majority of the business's income (80 per cent of revenue and nearly 100 per cent of profits) did not come from high-rollers, holidaying super-rich or Hollywood stars. It came from everyday visitors spending an average of US \$100 to \$500 per visit. By recognizing the lifetime value of its most loyal customers, and rewarding them on that basis, the business has been able to drive customer satisfaction – and repeat spending.

Questions related to your internal operations

There is some naturally some overlap between this and Chapter 4. However, while Chapter 4 is, in the most part, about data feeding directly to your internal systems, this section is about people interpreting data in order to make operations-related decisions. Thus, here you consider what you need to do internally to deliver your strategy. A big part of this is assessing which suppliers, distributers, partners or other intermediaries are crucial in delivering your strategy. It is also about your internal systems and competencies, and to what extent these are set up to deliver your strategic goals.

Operational business questions may include:

- Do we currently partner with the right people to deliver our strategy?

- What are our capacity bottlenecks?

- How do we optimize our supply chain?

- Are we getting the most out of our equipment or machinery?
- Which suppliers are most unreliable and why?
- Have we got the right IT systems in place?
- Which area of our business is exposed to most fraud?
- What parts of our operations could we make more efficient?
- What are the key quality issues we are experiencing?
- To what extent are our projects delivered on time and on budget?
- What is the environmental impact of our business and how can we reduce it?
- To what extent are we using our buildings in the most efficient way?

Let's look at project performance as an example – after all, most strategic and change initiatives are delivered via projects or programmes. It is therefore important to be able to understand project performance in terms of schedule, budget and quality of output. Project and programme analytics is the process of assessing how effective your internal projects and programmes have been so you can improve them in the future. Project and programme analytics will help you answer business questions like 'To what extent are our projects or programmes delivered on schedule?', 'To what extent are they delivered within budget?' and 'To what extent are they delivering the expected outcomes?'

Implementing a project or programme, no matter how big or small, without any follow-up assessment is a recipe for disaster and you will almost certainly run into difficulties. There are many ways for projects to fail. Famous examples include the new Wembley Stadium in London that opened in 2007 – four years later than planned. Or there's the iconic Sydney Opera House, which was scheduled to open in 1963 at a cost of AU \$7 million but actually opened in 1973 at a cost of AU \$102 million. The Channel Tunnel linking the UK and France went 80 per cent over budget, but that pales in comparison to Boston's 'Big Dig' tunnel construction project, which went 275 per cent or US \$11 billion over budget. By using project and programme analytics, companies can spot more quickly when things are heading off course and take corrective action. Or they can understand what made a project successful or unsuccessful and apply those insights to future projects. Both elements are critical if an organization is going to achieve its long-term goals.

I mentioned supply chain analytics in the previous chapter, as it's a particularly powerful way to use data. The purpose of supply chain analytics is to determine opportunities for savings, improvements or increased return while also ensuring that your customers get what they ordered as quickly as possible. By understanding what happens in your business between the moment you purchase from your suppliers to the moment your customers receive their goods, you can better control costs, price your products or services correctly, make money and keep your customers happy.

A real-life example of supply chain analytics comes from a major drinks manufacturer that I worked with. They were keen to better understand shrinkage rates across their supply chain, from production through to distribution to the retailers. In other words, they wanted to answer the question, 'Where are we losing the most products, either through breakages or theft?' The plan was to identify problem areas and institute processes or better packaging that would prevent this costly expense in future. As a result of some in-depth supply chain analytics – using tracking sensors, image analysis, interviews, etc – we identified that their supply chain was actually very secure. We discovered that the vast majority of their shrinkage occurred in the retail setting, where people were stealing the product from supermarkets. Based on this information, the company decided to work with the supermarkets to ensure better tagging of products, and thanks to this, they were able to reduce shrinkage considerably.

Questions related to your people

Your employees are probably your most important (perhaps even most expensive) asset. In some sectors, attracting the right people can be the key to competitive success. Assessing whether you have the right people on board, how to attract the best people, and then how to keep them therefore makes absolute business sense. Employee analytics can help you understand all this, and more, and provide the basis for key people-related decisions.

Your people-related business questions may include:

- What are our core competencies in the business?
- What skills gaps exist in our business at the moment?
- What key skills will we need in the next two years?
- How engaged are our employees?
- How effectively do we employ our people?
- To what extent do our people have spare capacity?
- How productive are our employees?
- What are our most successful recruitment channels?

- What are the most cost-effective recruitment channels for certain positions?
- What are the key reasons why employees are leaving?
- Which employees are at risk of leaving?
- Are the behaviours of our employees in line with the culture we want?
- How do our employees rate the leadership?

For example, employee churn analytics allows you to assess staff turnover rates and predict future turnover so you can intervene earlier and reduce employee churn. Hiring employees, training them, and then integrating them into the business and getting them up to speed costs time and money. When that investment is lost because too many employees are leaving the business, this can have a detrimental impact on product or service quality, customer satisfaction, morale, productivity and revenue – all of which can drastically impact the business's ability to achieve its strategic goals.

Employee churn analytics help you answer business questions such as 'How satisfied are our employees?' Historical employee churn rates can be useful as a benchmark but the real gold lies in comparing your business against industry averages, seeking to identify patterns. Perhaps most usefully, employee churn analytics can help you answer questions like 'Why are employees leaving?' and, once you know why, 'Which employees are at risk of leaving in future?' You can then take internal action to address issues and better engage employees.

Say you operate a knitwear business, for instance. You employ people who are highly skilled and they are increasingly difficult to replace if they leave. Recently they have been leaving in greater numbers and you are becoming alarmed so you conduct some employee churn analytics. You recruit an independent researcher to conduct exit interviews with employees from the last six months. You assume that these employees are being tempted away by the promise of high wages elsewhere. Your brand is strong and you know that employees are proud to work for the company but something is pulling them elsewhere. At least that's what you think.

The exit interview data is inconclusive. Even though the individuals have left, they are smart enough not to want to burn their bridges in a small town with limited employment so they say things like 'Oh it was time for a change', or 'I just wanted a new challenge'. However, when the researcher looked back at performance appraisal information and introduced social media data, a quite different picture emerged. Once particular manager on the factory floor was causing bottlenecks and then blaming his team when delivery deadlines were not met. The churn was largely down to this one individual and his negative impact far outweighed his positive impact. Based on this, you could decide to move him sideways in the organization, away from direct interaction with your skilled workforce.

A real-life example comes from Google. The company set out to find out whether managers really mattered (as opposed to the highly valued tech positions, which clearly mattered a great deal), by asking the simple question, 'Do managers actually make a positive impact at Google?' To answer this question, they looked at performance reviews and employee surveys to plot an overview of managers' performance on a graph.

It looked, on the whole, as though the managers were tightly clustered on the graph and all performing pretty well. So they cut that data into sections, looking specifically at the top quartile (best managers) and the bottom quartile (worst managers). They analysed how those best and worst managers performed, in terms of team productivity, how happy their employees were, how likely their employees were to stay with the company, etc. And the results were very surprising. Even though most of the managers appeared to be tightly clustered together on the graph, further investigation highlighted statistically significant differences between the best and worst managers in the cluster. This clearly answered the question: managers do have a positive impact at Google.

This was nice to know, but it didn't really change anything in the company. So they came up with a new question they wanted to answer: 'What makes a great manager at Google?' To answer the new question, they carried out two qualitative studies, one with direct reports and the other with managers. Based on this data, they came up with eight behaviours that made the biggest impact for managers at Google – things like 'is a good coach' and 'has a clear vision for the team'. The data also highlighted three behaviours that might cause a manager to struggle. All this could act as an early warning system to detect both great and struggling managers, and improve management performance across the organization.

Visualizing and communicating insights from data

When using data to make better decisions, the data user (or data customer, if you like) is a human being. The whole process is about people interpreting data in order to make smarter, more informed decisions. Remember, data is worth very little unless you can turn it into insights and action. This means it is very important to ensure it's as easy as possible to extract insights from the data. The easier it is to understand the data and pull out key insights, the easier it is for people to make decisions and act on that data. This is why data visualization and communication has become such a big topic in recent years. There are many different options for communicating data. These include simple graphics (like bar charts), written reports, commercial data visualization platforms that make the data attractive and easy to understand, and management dashboards that provide your people with the information they need whenever they need it.

Different audiences have different needs, both in terms of the types of data they need and how they will use it. Therefore, when thinking about disseminating and communicating data it is important to define who will have access to the data (or the insights from that data) – you need to define your data 'customers' and their requirements. For example, what format works best for your people? How will they access the information (web interface, reports, dashboards, etc)? How often? Knowing the answers to these questions will help you decide on the right visualization/communication tools for your business. I explore some examples of useful tools later in the chapter.

Should everyone have access to the data?

I recognize there is a dilemma around communicating data. Some of the most successful companies using data are successful precisely because everyone across the organization is invested in data, has access to data and uses it to inform their decisions. Ideally, then, you would look to give individuals across the company access to data so they can interrogate it themselves and make better decisions. However, in practice, this doesn't always work and some central coordination of data communications is advisable. Because people interpret data in different ways, you will need to recognize that they may need help extracting key messages. I therefore recommend a blended approach: widespread access to data across the company, where people are encouraged to use data as the basis for future business decisions, *as well as* a strong overarching corporate narrative that sets out key insights and trends, just to be sure that the most critical messages are understood by everyone.

There is an ever-growing plethora of tools and services designed to facilitate data analytics across the organization as a whole. This has given rise to the term 'citizen data scientist'. Retailer Sears, for example, recently enabled 400 staff from its business intelligence (BI) operations to carry out advanced, data-driven customer segmentation – work which would previously have been carried out by specialist analysts. The move is said to have created hundreds of thousands of dollars' worth of efficiencies in data preparation costs alone. It has also allowed them to make better decisions about what products are being shown to people as they use their websites.

Remember Dickey's Barbecue Pit and their Smoke Stack data system in Chapter 2? In that environment, getting end users to adopt the system and bring data into their everyday decision making was a big challenge – after all, many of their on-the-ground staff joined the company to become barbecue artisans, not data analysts. As Laura Rea Dickey explained:

> We have folks in very different, vertically integrated positions within the company. Those folks in the corporate office are based in a traditional office setting working around the reality of the business, all the way down to the folks in our stores on the front line who are running a barbecue pit and interacting with customers. Having a platform that can integrate with all of those different user types is probably our biggest challenge.

For Dickey's, the solution came in the form of a reporting dashboard that makes it easy for the whole spectrum of end users to access and understand the data. The fact that this dashboard is so easy to use means that it integrates far better into everyday operations. At the end of the day, data that is easy to access and understand is far more likely to translate into action.

Sprint, who we looked at earlier in this chapter, also use reporting dashboards as well as visualization tools to help staff get the most from data. As Jason Delker told me:

> The saying 'a picture is worth a thousand words' is even more true when it comes to data. Being able to use visualization tools allows people to understand very quickly what trends are happening, where the hotspots are – what things are succeeding and what things are failing – and that is invaluable.

This isn't to say that organizations will no longer have a need for highly educated and specialized data scientists; I think there will always be a need for data experts. But when achieving buy-in for data across the business is so important, what better way to achieve this than putting data in the hands of the people whose buy-in is needed?

Goodbye spreadsheet reporting, hello data visualization

It's fair to say we've entered big data's awkward teenage years, when more companies are getting on the data bandwagon and then using outdated tools to try to visualize and communicate that data; namely, spreadsheets. Surveys suggest that one in five businesses are using spreadsheets as their main tool to communicate data internally. There's nothing wrong with spreadsheets in themselves; they work extremely well for many different jobs. But data communication and visualization is not one of them.

According to a survey of 2,000 employees in the UK and United States, more than half of respondents said that knowing company performance data contributed significantly to their own positive performance.[1] In other words, employees want to be included in discussions about overall business performance, and that means that key data must be communicated across every level of the business. For that to work, businesses need something that can help them visualize the data more easily and effectively. Spreadsheets just aren't the right tool for that job. Important data is hidden in spread-sheets, meaning you're not seeing all the raw data at once, and this makes it hard to tell what's important and what's not. Visualization tools, however, can very clearly highlight the most important data or results. Also, spread-sheets are designed to store historical data, which makes it difficult, or even impossible, to spot trends over time and compare data across longer time periods. Visualization tools, on the other hand, are a great way to demon-strate trends.

The good news is that there are now many excellent and inexpensive tools available that allow companies to report data in more effective ways. Tools like Tableau and Qlik, to name just a couple, have helped bring data visualization to the masses. And Google has its powerful Analytics 360 suite, which allows enterprise teams to visualize data from multiple sources and create and share accessible reports and graphs. (They recently announced a free version of its Data Studio 360 product for smaller businesses and indi-viduals, too.) In addition, many commercial analytic platforms come with their own built-in visualization tools.

There is a significant shift underway at present. Not only are businesses beginning to really understand the importance of data, they are also under-standing the importance of communicating insights clearly to everyone in the organization. This is a great thing for the future of data; the better insights are communicated, the more likely it is that data leads to positive action (in this case, better business decisions).

Combining visuals and words for maximum impact

A picture can paint a thousand words, as the saying goes. In this way, visu-als are great for conveying information because they're quick and direct, they're memorable, and they add interest (being much more likely to hold the reader's attention than a full page of text). But unless we know how to decode its message, a picture can also be difficult to read. Words, on the other hand, usually have a very direct meaning and are simple to understand. With a short narrative, you can ensure everyone understands the data in the same way. This is why using visuals and narrative together is much more powerful than using either on their own. For instance, a graph detailing sales history is extremely useful for analysing trends over time, but a narrative can pull out the key messages and put that information into context – explaining what might be behind that trend, for example.

However, producing written narratives takes time and effort. And this makes the recently announced partnership between Qlik and Narrative Science so exciting. Narrative Science developed Quill, a powerful natural language processing tool, which is used across industries from finance to retail and even journalism to create detailed natural language reports from data. Quill's technology is ground-breaking. Not only is it able to interpret data, it can structure written words in a manner that is practically indistinguishable from those written by a human writer. And now users of the Qlik Sense BI platform can use Quill to create automated, intelligent narratives from their data and visualizations.

This means that visualizations can be used as a top layer to make the data more digestible. And the natural language processing tools then take the information a step further by adding another layer, a textual layer, which gives a handy explanation of the visualization. This is very impressive to see in action; a user simply interacts with visualized data through the Qlik Sense dashboard and, in real time, they will see a narrative write itself alongside the data. And it writes well, too, in simple language that is clear, concise and easy to understand. Given its power to make data easier to digest, I expect, in time, that this sort of functionality will become a standard feature of all good BI, analytics and visualization platforms.

Virtual reality and the future of data visualization

There has been a lot of very excited discussion recently around how virtual reality (VR) could affect the way we visualize data. There are inherent limitations in the amount of data that humans can absorb from a computer screen. In fact, according to SAS software architect Michael D Thomas, we are limited to processing less than 1 kilobit of information per second when reading text on a screen. Therefore, it's not much use having ever-growing amounts of processing power able to throw insights at us with ever-increasing speed, if we have no chance of keeping up.

This is where many people think virtual reality can help. By immersing the user in a digitally created space with a 360-degree field of vision and simulated movement in three dimensions, it should be possible to greatly increase the bandwidth of data available to our brains. This means we will be able to understand complex data more quickly and more accurately.

The fact is that the display interface we use to absorb data visually has long been due an overhaul. Screens may have got substantially smaller and lighter over the years, but essentially they are the same technology. While input, processing and storage capabilities have evolved iteratively throughout several generations of computing architecture, the screen itself, aside from increasing in definition and colour, has not. But this is changing, thanks to the emergence of more affordable VR hardware. In fact, the first of a wave of consumer VR headsets (Facebook's own Oculus Rift) hit the shelves just recently.

Some VR applications are already emerging which are geared towards data exploration and experimentation. Unity Studios, which produces one of the most widely used 3D game engines, is already exploring the use of its technology by business data analysts. As well as allowing increasingly sophisticated and granular visualization, the added level of immersion will undoubtedly be of great benefit in making sure the headline messages and key business insights hit home to users.

Endnote

1 Simon Whittick (2015) Research report: one in four employees leave due to mushroom management, *Geckoboard*, 21 September, available at: https://www. geckoboard.com/blog/research-report-one-in-four-employees-leave-due-to-mushroom-management/#.WGwINnoYPHF

Using data
to improve your
business operations

04

While the majority of businesses start by using data to enhance their decision making, data is becoming an increasingly important part of everyday business operations. At its core, this is about data helping businesses run more smoothly and efficiently – from the warehouse to customer services and everything in between. On a very basic level, this could involve human interaction with data, whereby the 'data customer' is a person who interprets data in order to improve operational processes and actions. But, increasingly, data-enhanced operations are less about humans working with data and more about machines themselves as data customers – and this is where I believe the real value of data lies, at least in terms of business operations. The real value comes from machines being able to collect quality data, automatically analyse that data and then act on what the data tells them. Machine-to-machine communication is a key element of this, enabling systems to work together to automate and improve processes, often without any human interaction at all. As we saw in Chapter 1, this has all become possible thanks to advances like sensors, the Internet of Things (IoT), machine learning, deep learning, artificial intelligence and robotics.

There are many ways data can enhance your operations but, broadly speaking, they fall into two main categories: 1) optimizing your everyday operational processes, ie how you run your business on a day-to-day basis, and 2) improving your customer offering, either through new or enhanced services, or better products. Whether you tackle both categories or just one will depend on your business. There are no hard-and-fast rules – operational improvements can be absolutely vital to a manufacturing company, for instance, but perhaps less business-critical to a services company. In this chapter, I explore both aspects in detail, along with plenty of real-world examples to give you an idea of the many possibilities.

Data is at its most powerful when it is helping an organization achieve its goals. Just as with data-based decision making (Chapter 3), data-based operations must be tied to your organization's business goals. Therefore, you need to look systematically at every layer of your operations to identify how optimizing processes and maximizing efficiencies can help achieve those goals – and then prioritize those opportunities accordingly. For most businesses, operational priority areas include manufacturing (eg monitoring equipment to identify wear and tear and reduce downtime), warehousing and distribution (eg automated stock control), business processes (eg detecting fraud), and sales and marketing (eg predicting customer churn).

Optimizing your operational processes with data

Using data, it is possible to optimize almost every aspect of how you run your business. Whether you want to improve your manufacturing processes by automatically detecting faults, optimize delivery routes, target the right customers, detect fraud quickly, or something else that helps you achieve your strategic goals, data can help. Indeed, businesses are already using data to increase efficiencies, reduce waste, streamline processes and increase revenue.

How data can improve the manufacturing process

Data plays a hugely important role in modern manufacturing processes. Data and analytics can, for example, be used for quality control, helping to identify faults in products before they hit the market. Data can help eliminate waste and drive continuous improvement processes. And it can even help increase product yield. In fact, one study showed a biopharmaceutical manufacturer was able to track the nine parameters that most affected yield variation for their vaccine.[1] Based on this data, they were able to increase yield by 50 per cent, leading to significant manufacturing savings on that product alone.

Understanding manufacturing performance is one of the most common ways data can enhance the manufacturing process. By embedding sensors into manufacturing equipment, you can capture valuable machine data that helps you monitor and measure the health and efficiency of those machines. Manufacturers around the world are already using this technology to manage their operations more efficiently and minimize downtime – which, in turn, helps them stay on top of productivity targets. Traditionally, manufacturing equipment is put on a time-based maintenance schedule, with machines being taken offline at certain times of the year to be checked over and for new parts to be installed on a 'just-in-case' basis (ie parts may be replaced according to the amount of time that has elapsed since they were fitted, as opposed to whether they really need replacing at that moment in time). These parts alone are expensive, but so is having the machine offline for several days at regular intervals. Sensors embedded in the machines, connected to particular parts or processes, can measure a wide variety of variables, such as temperature, pressure, movement, vibrations, proximity, light, and so on. The data is fed back to computers that monitor the machine's performance and flag up when a part needs to be replaced, or when the machine is running less than optimally and may be in need of a service. This real-time monitoring of machine data can create significant savings and increase output, allowing maintenance teams to fix problems before the machine breaks down, minimizing downtime caused by unnecessary servicing.

You can either install sensors into machines and equipment or you can leverage sensors that are already built into machines that you purchase. In many cases, it simply means connecting the machines to your IT system to collect and analyse the data. Many modern machines already have wireless connectivity via WiFi or Bluetooth and often come with software or apps to monitor and analyse the data, which makes the whole process a lot easier.

Sensors can also be embedded into the products you manufacture, in order to gather valuable data on product performance. Rolls-Royce is the prime example of a manufacturer leveraging such data to their advantage. The company manufactures nearly half the world's passenger jet engines and each of those engines is full of embedded sensors. These sensors monitor performance in real time, measuring some 40 parameters 40 times per second, including temperatures, pressures and turbine speeds. All the data is then stored in on-board computers and is simultaneously streamed via satellite back to Rolls-Royce HQ, where computers sift through the data to look for anomalies. If any are found, they are immediately flagged and a human being will check the results and, if necessary, telephone the airline and work out what needs to be done – often before the issue escalates into an actual problem. These sensors therefore allow for dynamic maintenance based on actual engine-by-engine performance, rather than some automatic rota system based on time alone. Instead of pulling an expensive piece of equipment out of service every three or six months, these sensors allow the airlines to maintain their fleet much more cost effectively and, more importantly, these sensors make the planes much safer. As well as improving engine maintenance, machine data has also led Rolls-Royce to change its business model too, providing a servicing revenue stream over and above their traditional manufacturing model – but more on that later in the chapter.

How data can enhance warehousing and distribution

Improving warehousing and distribution processes is one of the most obvious uses for data, precisely because it's a particularly data-rich business area. Almost every aspect of warehousing and distribution, from stock control to supply chain management to delivery routes (and a whole lot more), can be optimized using data. Even very traditional sectors can benefit from incorporating data into their operations. For example, I recently worked with a bus and coach company that were initially very sceptical about the value of data in their industry. Now they are collecting and analysing telematics data from their vehicles and using this data to improve driving behaviour, optimize transport routes and improve vehicle maintenance.

Supermarkets are using cameras and sensors to automatically monitor the quality of their fresh produce and identify problems with stock; using image data, computers can learn to identify vegetables that are starting to go bad, and sensors can pick up gases that are emitted from rotting fruit. This is just a small way in which the big supermarkets are using data to improve the way they operate. The savviest retailers are using data to predict product demand, build detailed customers profiles, manage stock levels, optimize deliveries, and increase sales through targeted product recommendations (more on some of these examples later in the chapter).

One of the best examples of optimized warehousing comes from an unsurprising source: Amazon. The company uses intricate computer systems to keep track of millions of stock items across dozens of warehouses and distribution centres around the globe. Amazon's newest UK warehouse, in Hemel Hempstead, holds millions of products across its 40,000 m^2 of warehouse. In an operation of this scale, efficiency is the key to success (particularly when you consider that, although Amazon's turnover is huge, its profits are relatively small. Low margins and incredibly high volumes are the order of the day, making efficiency even more important). Every product's progress through the warehouse is constantly monitored, from the moment it arrives from a supplier to the moment it is taken off the shelf by a (human – for now) picker to the moment it is labelled and dispatched to the end customer. At any one time, the company's systems can tell where exactly any one individual item is within the warehouse. Not only does this make for a more secure supply chain, it helps the company (and its warehouse staff) meet the very strict productivity targets that are necessary on this scale.

And Amazon is likely to automate the picking process even further – Amazon subsidiary Kiva Systems (bought by Amazon in 2012 for US $775 million) develops warehouse robotics like robotic shelves that move and bring products to stationary pickers before returning to their designated space in the warehouse. Warehouse robotics is an area Amazon is keen to develop, and the company has previously held competitions to find the best warehouse picker machines. The most recent competition was held in 2016, and robot entrants had to perform a number of tasks, including taking items of various shapes and sizes out of a box and putting them on the correct shelf, and taking items from a shelf and placing them in a box. This commitment to staying on top of the latest technology and constantly seeking new efficiencies is one of the reasons behind the company's success.

Back in the real-life Amazon warehouse, data and analytics are applied to much more than the picking process. Algorithms are used to automatically determine which size packaging is ideal for each product, saving time on packing and helping to eliminate waste from oversized packaging. And let's not forget that Amazon is already trialling drone deliveries, thereby automating the delivery process even further.

How data can enhance business processes

This is a broad category, covering any way in which data can streamline your everyday business processes, such as accounting or customer service. What this means for you depends very much on the industry within which you operate.

Data is particularly helpful when it comes to detecting fraud, from fraudulent credit card transactions to employee fraud to people lying on insurance claims. Fraud detection analytics uses data to identify patterns or certain behaviours that flag fraudulent activity, thereby enabling businesses to predict fraud and reduce or stop it. Fraud costs many businesses a great deal of money every year – global card fraud alone currently amounts to more than US $16 billion, and is predicted to top $35 billion in 2020. Online fraud is also a growing area that every business needs to be vigilant against.

Credit card companies and insurance firms are assessing for fraud on a constant basis. If you make an unusual purchase on your credit card, for instance, you will usually get a phone call or message from your credit card company to check the transaction is legitimate. This is because algorithms have assessed your normal credit card activity and geographic location and anything outside those (and many other) parameters raises a red flag.

One of my clients, a large insurance firm, is using voice analytics to detect potential fraudulent behaviour in customer calls. Their systems can identify stress levels in a customer's voice, which may sometimes indicate that the caller is not telling the truth. Of course, the person may be stressed because they've just had their home burgled, so the data is used to trigger further investigation, rather than as instant proof that the customer is lying! As an automatic early warning signal, however, it is extremely useful.

Car insurance companies are also using machine learning to analyse photos from car accidents in relation to injury claims. The computers can flag up when the injuries claimed are disproportionate to the vehicle damage sustained in the accident. Again, this is then used to trigger a more thorough investigation of the claim, rather than an instant rejection of the claim.

Insurance companies have also found a correlation between the time a customer takes to fill in their online claim form and fraud (ie either filling the form in too slowly or too quickly), and this data is now being routinely analysed by large insurers. Often when a customer takes too long to complete the form, or hovers over a field for too long, they are thinking too hard about what happened or what they should write. This can indicate they are not being entirely truthful about the event. Of course, this is not the only conclusion; insurance companies allow for the fact that sometimes the person may just be slow, or they may have been interrupted by the doorbell, or had to leave to pick the kids up from school. But the data raises a red flag that is collated with other data points, such as how many times a person changed the data in a particular field. If too many red flags are raised, the insurance assessor knows to look more closely at the case. Conversely, if the form is completed too quickly this can also raise alarm bells, because criminals often use bots to complete forms or they will cut and paste from previous claim forms to speed the process up.

Crucially, data analysis can not only help identify fraudulent activity, it can also help prevent fraud in future. Once fraudulent activity has been identified, it is possible to mine the data looking for patterns. This information can then be used to devise predictive models that highlight cases that are more likely to be fraudulent. So, when specific matches that are known to be indicative of fraud show up, the claim is flagged up for further investigation. These matches could involve the behaviour of the person making a claim, the network of people they associate with (through social media or other open sources of demographic data), or certain partner agencies involved in the claim (for example auto repair shops, where patterns of behaviour could indicate that a particular establishment is involved in underhand activity which a claimant may be complicit in).

Even businesses not operating in high-fraud areas like finance and insurance can benefit from fraud detection. You can, for example, use CCTV footage to monitor warehouses and picking and packing areas, and use video analytics to flag potentially fraudulent activity.

Assessing risk is another area in which data is particularly valuable. Predictive, statistical modelling basically means working out what will happen in the future by measuring and understanding as much as we possibly can about what has happened in the past. Models are then built that show what is likely to happen in the future, based on the relationships between variables as demonstrated in past data – all of which helps businesses establish how likely something is to happen and the level of risk. Predictive modelling is a key tool in the world of big data, and the insurance industry (predictably) has been very keen to adopt it.

One of the most important uses is for setting policy premiums. Insurers must set the price of premiums at a level which ensures them a profit by covering their risk, but also fits with the budget of the customer – otherwise they will go elsewhere. To price premiums appropriately, insurers must be able to accurately assess the risk posed by particular drivers.

Many insurers now offer telemetry-based packages (often through an app on the customer's phone), where actual driving information is fed back to their system in order to build a personalized, highly accurate profile of an individual customer's driving behaviour. Using predictive modelling, the insurer can work out an accurate assessment of that driver's likelihood to be involved in an accident, or have their car stolen, by comparing their behavioural data with that of thousands of other drivers in their database.

The idea behind all of these initiatives is that the ability to accurately assess risk and spot fraudulent activity results in lower costs and increased efficiencies across the insurance industry – and for the average safe driver this translates to lower premiums and a better, more personalized service from their insurer.

The applications of data go way beyond assessing risk and fraud, however. For example, data, machine learning and natural language processing are helping media companies generate content more quickly and efficiently. In Chapter 3 we looked at Narrative Science, the company that provides tools for natural language processing and text generation. Narrative Science's software can automatically analyse a company's financial performance data and generate an article or financial report that is indistinguishable from one written by a human writer. In fact, Narrative Science's work is so good, the company now writes articles for *Forbes* (and I genuinely cannot tell the difference between Narrative Science articles and those written by journalists).[2] For any company that relies on fast, efficient and accurate content generation, natural language tools like this can be a game changer. But the applications extend to companies in any industry. For example, large organizations spend a great deal of time and money creating in-depth financial performance reports, and these can now be generated automatically by computers. And natural language processing software has the advantage over human writers because it enables content to be quickly and easily customized – so different versions of the same report can be produced for different audiences.

Data and analytics are even helping cities fight crime more efficiently. ShotSpotter technology, developed by US company SST Inc, analyses the entire soundscape of a city and provides real-time alerts when gunfire is detected. It works by using sound sensors positioned at strategic locations in neighbourhoods with high levels of gun crime. When a soundwave which matches the profile of gunfire is detected by three sensors, then its precise location can be ascertained by measuring the difference in time it takes for the sound to reach each sensor. Having rolled out the technology in 90 cities around the world, the company has recently announced a partnership with GE, which will see ShotSpotter technology installed into all GE Intelligent LED Smart City street lights. The early signs are very encouraging; cities that have already deployed the technology have seen a reduction in gun crime of 28 per cent – and the value as a deterrent is huge.

In European cities, where gun violence is far less of an issue than in the United States, the technology could be applied to counter-terrorism. In South Africa, ShotSpotter has been successfully used to help capture poachers targeting endangered rhinos in the Kruger National Park. And in Southeast Asia, a modified version of the system is being used to fight blast fishing, which is causing irreparable damage to coral reefs.

How data can enhance sales and marketing processes

Data and analytics can also help automate and optimize certain sales and marketing processes, such as personalized recommendations for customers and dynamic pricing. One client of mine, a leading telecoms company, is using analytics to predict customer satisfaction and potential customer churn. Based on phone and text patterns, along with social media data, the company is able to automatically classify customers into different categories based on how likely they are to cancel their contract and switch to a competitor. Using this data, the company is able to closely monitor the satisfaction levels of certain customers and prioritize actions to prevent them cancelling their contracts.

I have done a lot of work with leading retailers over the past few years, and it is safe to say that big data analytics is now being applied at every stage of the retail process: working out what the popular products will be by predicting trends, forecasting where the demand will be for those products, optimizing pricing for a competitive edge, identifying the customers likely to be interested in the products and working out the best way to approach them, taking their money and finally working out what to sell them next.

In the case of optimized pricing, data helps companies identify when prices should be dropped – known as 'mark-down optimization'. Before in-depth analytics became available, most retailers simply reduced prices at the end of a buying season, by which point demand had practically disappeared. However, analytics has shown that a more gradual reduction in price, from the moment demand starts to sag, generally leads to increased revenues. Experiments by US retailer Stage Stores found that this approach, backed by a predictive approach to determine the rise and fall of demand for a product, beat a traditional 'end of season sale' approach 90 per cent of the time. Macy's adopts a similar approach, changing pricing frequently to react to retail trends and demand. The system has proven to be much more efficient than previous pricing models – reportedly, the retailer has been able to save 26 hours every time it optimizes pricing for its 73 million products.

Walmart, the largest retailer in the world and the world's largest company by revenue, is a 'traditional' bricks-and-mortar retailer that clearly understands the value of data. In 2015, the company announced it was in the process of creating the world's largest private data cloud, to enable the processing of 2.5 petabytes of information every hour. Supermarkets compete not just on price but also on customer service and convenience. Having the right products in the right place at the right time presents huge logistical problems, and products have to be efficiently priced to the cent to stay competitive. Walmart works with a constantly refreshed database consisting of 200 billion rows of transactional data – and that only represents the most recent few weeks of business! On top of that it pulls in data from 200 other sources, including meteorological data, economic data, telecoms data, social media data, gas prices and a database of events taking place in the vicinity of Walmart stores. All of this data is used to determine which products people are most likely to want, and where, and what is the most competitive price. Another initiative is Walmart's Social Genome Project, which monitors public social media conversations and attempts to automatically predict what products people will buy based on their online conversations.

When it comes to optimizing online sales through data and analytics, Amazon – more specifically, Amazon's recommendation engine – is the benchmark. Amazon probably didn't invent the recommendation engine but they certainly introduced it to widespread public use.

Amazon gathers data on every one of their over a quarter of a billion customers while they use the site, and this data is used to build and continually fine-tune the recommendation engine. The theory is that the more they know about you, the more likely they are to be able to predict what you want to buy. As well as what you buy, Amazon monitors what you look at, your shipping address (to determine demographic data – they can take a good stab at guessing your income level by knowing what neighbourhood you live in) and whether you leave customer reviews and feedback. They also look at the time of day you are browsing, to determine your habitual behaviours and match your data with others who follow similar patterns. All of this data is used to build up a 360-degree view of individual customers. Based on this, Amazon can find other people who they think fit into the same niche (employed males between 18 and 45 living in a rented house with an income of over US $30,000 who enjoy foreign films, for example) and make recommendations based on what others in that group like.

The big lesson here is the more a business (any business) knows about a customer, the better it can sell to them. Developing a 360-degree view of each customer as an individual is the foundation of data-driven marketing and sales.

Using data to improve your customer offering

As well as improving your business operations, data can also help you improve your customer offering by delivering a better service or product. This can mean adding extra value for customers by enhancing existing products or services through the use of data, or it can mean creating a whole new customer value proposition. Again, how you use data in relation to your customer offering will depend on your business's strategic goals. Data for data's sake is never a great idea – instead, focus on the areas that help your business grow and get to where it needs to be.

Delivering a better service to customers

Let's revisit Rolls-Royce briefly. Remember the sensors they put in their jet engines? These sensors continuously monitor the performance of more than 3,700 jet engines worldwide to identify issues before they arise. The data generated by these sensors has led Rolls-Royce to alter its business model. While the company used to simply manufacture and sell the engines, they have now created ongoing revenue streams over and above their manufacturing business. As well as selling the engines, Rolls-Royce now offers to monitor them on an ongoing basis, and repair or replace parts if there is a problem, charging customers based on engine usage time – they have 'servitized' their product offering by adding a data-based service element to their products. The client is effectively buying a dynamic servicing option, which helps them run their own operations more efficiently and safely (because aircraft maintenance can be better planned and scheduled). That's great for the clients, but it also translates into a significant revenue bump for Rolls-Royce – servicing now accounts for a massive 70 per cent of the civil aircraft engine division's annual revenue.

Similarly, US agricultural manufacturer John Deere has embraced big data enthusiastically, launching several big data-enabled services which let farmers benefit from crowdsourced, real-time monitoring of data collected from its thousands of users. Myjohndeere.com is an online portal which allows farmers to access data gathered from sensors attached to their own machinery as they work the fields, as well as aggregated data from other users around the world. It's also connected to external data sets including weather and financial data. These services allow farmers to make more informed decisions about how to use their equipment, where they will get the best results from, and what return on their investment they are providing. Another John Deere service is Farmsight, launched in 2011, which allows farmers to make decisions about what crops to plant where, based on information gathered in their own fields and those of other users.

Data is helping healthcare providers offer a more efficient and personalized service to patients. IBM's Watson platform is focusing a lot on the healthcare industry, and IBM claim that it can analyse vast quantities of data more accurately than human specialists while reducing costs.[3] Naturally, this creates a lot of potential to automate and speed up certain services. IBM is also working on an interface that would allow Watson (or a program like it) to analyse the existing medical research on any given topic and then summarize the information for the doctor. The doctor would then be able to make the best treatment choices for an individual patient based on the vast amounts of data available – without having to spend hours doing the research himself. It's likely that the medicines and treatments the doctor would then prescribe will also have been developed with the aid of data. Recently, data-sharing arrangements between the pharmaceutical giants has led to breakthroughs such as the discovery that Desipramine, commonly used as an anti-depressant, has potential uses in curing types of lung cancer.

Transport for London (TfL) is also using data to provide a better service to customers. The company oversees London's network of buses, trains, taxis, roads, cycle hire bikes, cycle paths, footpaths and even ferries which are used by millions every day. Running these vast networks gives TfL access to huge amounts of data – and the company is using this data to plan services and provide better information to customers.

Big data analysis also helps TfL respond when disruption occurs. When something unexpected happens, for example if TfL's services are affected by a signal failure, the company can measure how many people are delayed so that customers can apply for refunds. When the disruption is particularly severe, TfL can automatically give refunds to affected customers. Customers travelling with a contactless payment card will have their travel automatically credited to their account. When there are longer-term planned disruptions, TfL uses historical patterns to judge where customers are likely to be headed to and plan alternative services to meet that demand. Travel data is also used to identify customers who regularly use specific routes and send tailored travel updates to them, letting them know how they'll be affected by disruption.

Lauren Sager Weinstein, head of analytics at TfL, gave me a specific example when Wandsworth Council was forced to close Putney Bridge – where buses carried 110,000 journeys over the bridge each week – for emergency repairs:

> We were able to work out that half of the journeys started or ended very close to Putney Bridge. The bridge was still open to pedestrians and cyclists, so we knew those people would be able to cross and either reach their destination or continue their journey on the other side. Either they lived locally or their destination was local. The other half were crossing the bridge at the halfway point of their journey. In order to serve their needs, we were able to set up a transport interchange and increase bus services on alternate routes. We also sent personalized messages to all those travelling in the area about how their journey was likely to be affected.

Data and analytics are even helping city councils run public services more efficiently, and provide a better service to residents and improve their quality of life. Milton Keynes in the UK is a great example of a 'smart city', using smart, connect technology to improve public utilities. This subject is quite close to my heart, not least because 'smart cities' will be a big topic in the next few years, but also because Milton Keynes is my home town. Over the next 10 years or so, an extra 50,000 people are expected to move to Milton Keynes, boosting the population from 0.25 million to 0.3 million. Even for a young town like Milton Keynes, with a relatively modern infrastructure, this is likely to cause some problems in the delivery of public services.

To counter this, the town council has been exploring how smart, connected, data-driven technology can help improve public services. Geoff Snelson, director of strategy at Milton Keynes Council and lead on the programme, told me, 'We've got sensors being deployed into recycling bins that show when they're full, into car parking spaces, and into some of our local parks, which show footfall and things like water temp and soil moisture.' For example, a sensor network has been rolled out across all 80 of the council's neighbourhood recycling centres to help streamline collection services, so wagons can prioritize the fullest recycling centres and do not need to travel to those with almost nothing in them.

In addition, homes are being used to test a variety of energy-saving technology, and soon driverless cars will be trialled on the town's streets. By the end of the three-year trial period, the hope is these driverless cars will be mingling with (and hopefully avoiding) people-driven cars in sections of the town. Another project involves taking high-definition satellite imagery and overlaying it with data from the planning department to make sure the town is growing in the correct manner, in line with planning guidelines and local growth plans. As Snelson put it, 'A lot of these solutions are about delivering efficiencies by gathering better – more timely and more accurate – information. It's not voodoo – just better information.'

Delivering a better product

Thanks to technological advances, specifically the ever-increasing interconnectivity the IoT brings, data can also help you optimize the very products you offer, and how your customers use them.

One brilliant example comes from the huge array of smart devices that is now available for the average home. I have a smart TV which can detect when my young children enter the room and automatically switch off any non-child-friendly programmes. I also have a smart Nest fire alarm which is connected to smart security cameras and my smart thermostat. So if the fire alarm goes off while I'm not home, I can log in and see from the cameras what is happening. Assuming it's a false alarm, I can turn off the alarm remotely from my phone.

Nest serves as a great example of an IoT-based business which is coming up with products that have the potential to simplify or improve our lives. Nest Labs was bought by Google in 2014 for US $3.2 billion – a big indicator of how key this market is likely to be in future. It's clear that Google expects its services to be the powerhouse behind the smart homes of the future, and that it sees Nest's products as some of the first building blocks behind the 'operating system' that we will use to interact with those homes.

All of this is part of the ongoing spread of the IoT into our everyday lives. We now have Ralph Lauren producing smart polo shirts that pick up the wearer's movement data, as well as breathing and heart rates. SmartMat have produced the world's first smart yoga mat, which detects when users are out of alignment and gives real-time feedback on how to correct their pose. Pantelligent's smart frying pan features a temperature sensor that communicates with an app on your phone and tells you when you need to flip your steak or when the temperature is too high.

Even Mattel, working in partnership with ToyTalk, is getting in on the act with its new AI-driven Barbie doll. Called Hello Barbie, the doll has a microphone concealed in her necklace that records what anyone says to her and transmits it to the servers at ToyTalk. There, the recording is parsed, analysed, and the correct response selected and sent back for Barbie to deliver – all in under a second. Every one of Barbie's potential conversations is mapped out, like the branches of a tree, with more than 8,000 lines of dialogue available to her as possible responses. Barbie also remembers what children say, storing answers to be used later in conversation. If, for example, your child says her favourite singer is Taylor Swift, Barbie will remember and mention that a few days or weeks later. (Updates will be recorded periodically so that Barbie is always up to date on the latest pop culture.)

As you might imagine, the doll isn't a hit with everyone and there are concerns about how the conversational data is being used. All of the child's responses are recorded and stored on ToyTalk's servers, where parents and employees of ToyTalk, Mattel, and their undisclosed partners can listen back to the conversations. ToyTalk has said in a statement that the data collected will not be used for advertising purposes, but the potential is certainly there. (Theoretically, Hello Barbie could let your child know when Taylor Swift's new album is out or when concert tickets go on sale, for example.) And, as The Campaign for Commercial-Free Childhood asserts, 'Even parents shouldn't listen to secret recordings of their children!'

Misgivings or no, it's likely Hello Barbie is just one in a long line of AI-enabled products that will take advantage of deep learning algorithms to interact with us in more and more realistic ways in future. Google, for example, is already predicting that we will eventually use voice commands more than typing on our mobile devices.

The development of smart products like sports shirts, yoga mats and dolls is a clear sign that every industry is waking up to the potential benefits of smart, data-driven innovation, and no one wants to be left out. Effectively, all businesses are becoming data businesses – even the ones you'd least expect. When almost any product can be connected to the Internet and other products, there is huge potential to improve product offerings – and for the mountain of data being generated to feed back into the business, helping to provide a better service and streamline operations.

The really exciting thing (or scary thing, depending on your point of view) is that the developments outlined in this chapter are just the warm-up act. The technology is evolving very quickly and we're at the beginning of a data revolution that has the potential to impact almost every product, service and business. The future will see all of these strands come together – machine-to-machine communication, machine learning, robotics, AI, automated monitoring and remote monitoring of our homes, driverless cars, automatic cancer scanning, etc – to create a very different world.

As the connectivity of objects increases, smart homes, smart cities, and even smart countries will become the norm. And, as the number of devices connected to the Internet is soon to exceed the number of humans on the planet, the real value clearly lies in machines being able to communicate and exchange information with each other, and analyse that information in real time. As machine learning capabilities increase, and machines get better at learning from data and modifying their actions based on what the data tells them, *without any human input*, we are likely to see some very interesting developments in the not-too-distant future.

Endnotes

1 Louis Columbus (2014) Ten ways big data is revolutionizing manufacturing, *Forbes*, 28 November, available at: http://www.forbes.com/sites/louiscolumbus/2014/11/28/ten-ways-big-data-is-revolutionizing-manufacturing/#747b95627826

2 You can find the *Forbes* articles contributed by Narrative Science at: http://www.forbes.com/sites/narrativescience/#117a32554f72

3 Ian Steadman (2013) IBM's Watson is better at diagnosing cancer than human doctors, *Wired*, 11 February, available at: http://www.wired.co.uk/article/ibm-watson-medical-doctor

Monetizing your data

05

Increasingly, data is becoming a key business asset in its own right, and the ability to monetize data successfully can transform a business's overall value and the bottom line. A glance at the 10 most valuable Fortune 500 companies proves this; in 2016, according to Fortune.com, four of the top five most valuable companies have either built their entire business model on data, or are heavily investing in data: Apple, Alphabet (Google's parent company), Microsoft and Facebook are all in the top five. Amazon also joined the top 10 in 2016, jumping to ninth place from its previous ranking of 19. While all five companies can be loosely lumped together in the 'tech' basket, they operate in different fields and with different business models: Microsoft is a software giant, Apple manufactures some of the most iconic products in the world, Amazon is a retailer, Facebook is a social network platform, and Google (despite its many different strands) is, at its heart, a media company. What unites these companies is their ability to gather and harness huge amounts of data to their advantage. It's likely that data-based companies will continue to squeeze traditional industrial behemoths out of the top 10.

There are two aspects of monetizing data: one is data's ability to increase the overall value of a company, and the other is an organization's ability to create extra value from data by selling that data back to customers or other interested parties. We saw some brief examples of companies successfully monetizing data in Chapter 2, but in this chapter I explore both options in more detail.

From a data strategy point of view, as discussed in Chapters 3 and 4, the key is to focus on the data that is right for your business, ie the data that brings the organization closer to realizing its long-term business goals. Rarely is it a good idea to collect as much data as possible in the hope that it will prove valuable one day. Some companies do make a success of the 'collect everything' approach but they are usually either data brokers, whose primary business function is to collect data and sell it to third parties, or companies with such huge budgets and manpower that they can cope with large volumes of data. For most organizations, however, a more focused, thoughtful approach to data is advisable.

Thus, the process of monetizing data starts with taking a big step back and asking yourself, 'What data is important to us as a business or to potential data customers?' Only once you have answered that question can you begin to consider whether that data can be monetized in other ways. The two questions you're looking to answer at this stage are, 'Can we use our data to make the company more valuable?' and 'Can we sell this data elsewhere?' The examples in this chapter will help you look for similar monetization opportunities in your own organization, but the ultimate goal is to make the very most of your data and create as much value as possible from it – in whatever way works best for your company. With this in mind, some organizations find it helpful to create a separate business unit charged with identifying and maximizing opportunities to monetize data. This is certainly a sensible approach and something that will become more common in medium and large organizations over the next few years.

Increasing the value of your organization

Companies are being bought and sold for the data they own, or their ability to work with data. IBM's US $2 billion acquisition of The Weather Company is a great example, and this savvy acquisition has given IBM access to The Weather Company's huge data sets – data which, as we saw in Chapter 2, can be of vital importance to a wide range of businesses and industries. Similarly, Microsoft's purchase of LinkedIn gives them access to the professional network's user data, and this data has the potential to help Microsoft personalize its collaboration and productivity tools, making Microsoft more competitive in the enterprise market. But it's not just obvious tech or data companies who can boost their value with data. Utah-based genealogy website Ancestry.com sold in 2012 for a reported US $1.6 billion. Why? Because the company had amassed so much personal data on their two million paying subscribers.

When data itself is the core business asset

There's no doubt that data itself can be incredibly valuable, so much so that it becomes a company's biggest asset. Let's look at a recent example of data drastically impacting the value of a company. UK Supermarket chain Tesco has a popular loyalty card scheme, named the Clubcard, which reportedly has 16 million members. The scheme proved so popular with customers it helped Tesco overtake Sainsbury's as the UK's biggest supermarket in 1999. The Clubcard allows Tesco to collect mountains of data on who customers are, where they live, and what products they buy – all of which helps them build up detailed customer profiles and created targeted offers.

The loyalty card programme, and all its data and analytics, is run by a third-party company called Dunnhumby (which also works with other retail partners like Macy's). Dunnhumby's volume of data and ability to extract customer insights was so valuable to Tesco they bought a stake in the company in 2001. In 2006, Tesco increased that stake to 84 per cent. The value of Dunnhumby continued to grow and, amid tough retail conditions in the UK and plummeting profits, Tesco decided to sell Dunnhumby in late 2014. The price tag? A whopping £2 billion. At one point, even Google Ventures were mooted as a potential buyer. However, the potential value of the sale dropped to just £700 million in 2015 after Dunnhumby lost access to data from US retailer Kroger (another one of their previous retailer partners). Things got more complicated when Tesco's own data was factored in, because most of Dunnhumby's profit reportedly comes from re-selling Tesco's data to companies like Coca-Cola. If Tesco sold the company, they would either become another Dunnhumby client, or take their data elsewhere – and, unsurprisingly, this put potential buyers off even more. After a 'comprehensive strategic review', Tesco decided to scrap the sale in late 2015. All of this goes to show how much of the company's value came from its data. Without Tesco's data, the value of Dunnhumby boils down to its people and technology – in other words, its ability to work with data. The ability to work with data can be incredibly valuable and attractive to buyers, as we'll see later in the chapter, but not to the tune of £2 billion – or even £700 million – in this case.

Direct marketing firm Acxiom are sometimes referred to as 'the biggest company you've never heard of'. The company revolutionized the US direct marketing industry in the 1980s by applying advanced analytics to massive data sets, long before the term 'big data' became so widespread. According to the company's website, they hold data on 'all but a small percentage' of US households – an impressive claim, and not bad for a company that started by managing a simple mailing list for the local Democratic party.

In the 1980s, Acxiom created their own proprietary list order fulfilment system, which took data from credit agencies and combined it with the first online mailing list generator. This provided businesses with millions of unique, named leads, segmented by age, location, profession, industry or any other known information, even down to what magazines people subscribed to. Just one of Acxiom's databases could hold data on 100 million people.

Acxiom take their data from public records such as electoral rolls, marriage and birth registers, credit agencies, consumer surveys, and from thousands of other businesses and organizations that collect data on their customers and service users, and pass it on (when those customers fail to 'opt out' of their data being shared!).

After pioneering data-driven marketing, Acxiom have moved with the times. In 2010, they unveiled their PersonicX system, which analyses a person's public social media activity (which is becoming a very useful source of insights into consumer sentiment and behaviour) to match them to particular consumer profiles. Combining this with their other data, Acxiom can more precisely match people with products and services they may need. Acxiom sell these services to businesses around the world, from small businesses right up to global financial giants. As a result, the company grew from originally employing 27 people to over 7,000 people. Today, Acxiom reportedly generate 12 per cent of the entire US direct marketing industry, which amounts to a significant annual turnover. Indeed, the company generated US $1.020 billion in 2015.

Experian are best known for providing credit references, which are used by banks and financial services companies to help them decide whether to lend people money. They also provide a range of other services based around the data they have collected, such as fraud and identity theft protection. More recently, they have added specialized data-analytics-driven services aimed at helping business customers in the automobile trading, healthcare insurance and small business markets.

Experian hold around 30 petabytes of data on people all over the world in their credit bureau database, which is currently growing at a rate of 20 per cent annually. They collect their data on individuals from lenders, who give them details on how much people borrow and whether they make repayments, as well as links between addresses that people have moved from and to, and any aliases used. They also harvest large amounts of data from public records, such as postal address databases, electoral registers, county court registers, birth and death records (to establish if fraud is being committed in the name of a deceased person) and national fraud prevention services such as the UK's Cifas system.

All this data is used to build up a detailed picture of consumers and businesses. As well as holding detailed data on individuals, such as their credit history, and demographic information such as age, location and income status, Experian group individuals into one of 67 types and 15 groups using their socio-demographic tool Mosaic. These groups include 'urban cool' (successful city dwellers owning or renting expensive apartments in fashionable city locations), 'professional rewards' (experienced professionals with successful careers living in financial comfort in rural or semi-rural areas), and 'global fusion' (young working people in metropolitan terraces with a wide variety of ethnic backgrounds). This segmented customer data is used for marketing purposes as well as to assess creditworthiness and insurability.

Experian have said that by integrating data analysis across the entirety of their operation, and treating all of their data as a centralized pool rather than as separate, segregated resources, they are enabling more people to buy homes, expand their businesses and manage their finances effectively. And the value of all this to Experian is huge, amounting to US $4.8 billion in revenue in 2015.

What these examples have in common is the sheer volumes of data that they're working with. The Tesco data set is by far the smallest, with around 16 million customers on record. It's these massive data sets that have made the companies so valuable. For many organizations, gathering data on this scale is simply out of the question. However, it is worth remembering that Acxiom and Experian both mine data from external sources (I talk more about the differences between internal and external data and the different data sources in Chapter 6), which means they are effectively making use of other people's data. These days it is possible to buy in or access data on almost anything or any group of people. And that opens up a world of opportunities for businesses.

When the value lies in a company's ability to work with data

Data in its own right can significantly boost the value of a company, but so can a company's ability to extract value from data. Data is especially valuable when it's combined with sophisticated systems, apps and algorithms to extract important insights from data. For example, we saw in Chapter 1 that pizza delivery company Domino's captures a lot of customer data and uses that data to improve its marketing. Having solid data systems like this in place, and having the ability to work with data, makes the company more valuable and attractive as a whole. The value of Domino's, for example, is likely to be significantly higher than a comparable pizza delivery company that isn't using data effectively.

In this way, companies are being bought for their ability to turn data into insights that lead to business growth. Google, for example, bought UK-based AI firm DeepMind in 2014 for more than US $500 million because of the company's deep learning capabilities. Google knew these capabilities could help them make better use of their data and gain competitive advantage over other tech giants. It is one of many data-related acquisitions Google has made in recent years, including the acquisition of Nest Labs and their smart products, discussed in Chapter 4.

Similarly, Facebook acquired Israeli facial recognition firm Face.com in 2012, in order to integrate Face.com's facial recognition capabilities into the social network. It is this technology that allows Facebook to automatically scan faces in the photos that users upload and suggest names, so users no longer have to manually tag their friends. Simplifying the tagging process for users and increasing the network's ability to recognize individuals is entirely in Facebook's interests. After all, a tagged photo is more useful to Facebook than an untagged photo because it is more likely to be seen by a larger number of users (ie everyone who is friends with the people tagged in the photo, as well as friends of the person who uploaded the photo). And encouraging users to post more photos is a good thing because it nets Facebook a whole lot more data: who people are with, where they are, perhaps even what brands and products they like (the technology already exists to identify specific products in photographs).

The key takeaway here is that, even if you aren't amassing huge amounts of data, the ability to gather and analyse the *right data* for your business could well help boost the overall value of the company and make it more attractive to investors or buyers in the long term.

Selling data to customers or interested parties

Companies are increasingly creating extra revenue streams by selling access to their data, or partnering with other interested parties who can make use of their data. Tesco's Clubcard data is a prime example of this, with Dunnhumby selling customer-based insights to consumer goods companies like Coca-Cola. However, this doesn't have to mean selling data on individuals or customer groups. Sometimes highly specialized or niche data can be incredibly valuable. John Deere, for example, creates extra revenue by selling farmers access to data on machinery performance, soil conditions, crops and yield. This data is only useful to a specific audience, but, for that audience, it's vital information.

When working with data – any kind of data – it therefore makes sense to consider whether there are any opportunities to create additional value from that data. The potential is there in almost any industry. A hotel booking site, for instance, could sell an enhanced package to hotels that gives them pricing recommendations, access to customer segment information or insights on what makes a customer more likely to book with them (reviews, photographs, most desired amenities, etc). A car manufacturer could partner with insurance companies to provide data on how many miles drivers do, where they travel to most frequently, whether they travel on roads with high accident rates, and how fast they drive on average. Companies who manufacture any kind of machinery can build sensors into those machines to provide extra insights for those who buy and use the machines (just as John Deere have done). These days, sensors are tiny and relatively inexpensive, which means they can be built into almost any product – even shirts and yoga mats, as we saw in Chapter 4. And the data generated from these sensors can potentially be sold back to customers (perhaps via an enhanced version of an app) or aggregated and sold to other companies.

With iPhones and iPads already in the hands of millions, Apple is no stranger to leveraging user-generated data, and has been keen to build partnerships and encourage the development of apps that are based on monitoring and sharing user data. Apple has recently partnered with IBM to facilitate the development of health-related mobile apps. The partnership allows iPhone and Apple Watch users to share data with IBM's Watson Health cloud-based healthcare analytics service, giving IBM's data-crunching engines access to real-time activity and biometric data from potentially millions of people who use Apple's devices around the world. Apple has also provided a range of applications targeted at other industries, including air travel, education, banking and insurance, also developed in partnership with IBM and aimed at bringing analytical capabilities to users of its mobile devices in those fields. The Apple Watch will accelerate this process even further – analysts estimate that around 12 million Apple Watches were sold in the first year since launch. Designed to be worn all day long, and to collect a wider variety of data thanks to additional sensors, the Apple Watch means even more personal data is available for analysis, and the potential to capitalize on this extra data through additional services and partnerships is huge.

All the major credit card companies have divisions that focus on selling transactional data to interested businesses, and this creates millions of dollars in additional revenue for Visa, Mastercard and American Express every year. Credit card companies have access to really quite sophisticated data – far more so than individual retailers. This means that, while Tesco may know exactly what I purchase in their store, Visa knows an awful lot more about who I am, where I go, what I buy, and what my monthly spend profile is.

American Express handles more than 25 per cent of credit card activity in the United States, and the company interacts with people on both sides of transactions: millions of businesses and millions of buyers. It therefore comes as no surprise that American Express is increasingly moving away from focusing on its traditional function of providing credit for consumers and merchant services for processing transactions, and towards actually making the connection between consumers and the businesses that want to reach them. As such, American Express is offering new online business trend analysis and industry peer benchmarking based on anonymized data to help companies see how they are doing compared with their competition. Amex removes any personally identifiable data from the transactions, but is still able to provide retailers with detailed trends within specific niche markets or customer segments. The company is on the leading edge of integrating data collection and analysis and machine learning into its business model and practices. Other credit card companies such as MasterCard and Visa are applying similar technologies and integrating them into their business models.

Remember Google Nest and its range of smart thermostats and security devices for the home? Not only does Google benefit from more detailed data on our individual homes, it's also profiting by partnering with utilities companies. Many energy providers are offering deals such as free thermostats to home owners, on the condition they give permission for the companies to take control of them at certain times, to cope with peaks and drops in demand on energy from the network. And the energy companies pay Nest around US $50 for each customer who signs up to these deals – which is more than worth it as far as the energy companies are concerned because they can make significant savings by regulating usage at peak times.

Facebook, too, is a master of monetizing user-generated data. Because websites are hosted on computers, not newspapers or billboards, each visitor can be independently identified by the software running the website. And Facebook, with around 1.5 billion active monthly users, has access to far more user data than just about anyone else. Its data is also more personal – whereas services like Google can track our web page visits (which incidentally Facebook can now also do) and infer much about us from our browsing habits, Facebook often has full access to demographic data such as where we live, work, play, how many friends we have, what we do in our spare time and the particular movies, books and musicians we like. Data collected by users as they browse Facebook is used to match them with companies which offer products and services that, statistically, they are likely to be interested in. A book publisher, for example, can pay Facebook to put their adverts in front of a million people who like similar books, and match the demographic profiles of their customers. Facebook's tactic of leveraging their huge wealth of consumer data to sell advertising space is clearly paying off. In 2014, Facebook took a 24 per cent share of the US online display ads market and generated US $5.3 billion in revenue from ad sales. By 2017 this has been forecasted to be a 27 per cent share, worth over US $10 billion.

Uber is one company whose everyday operations rely on big data. Everything from assessing demand to setting prices is governed by data. But Uber is also starting to generate extra revenue by selling that data to interested parties. The company hasn't revealed exactly how many customers it has, but we do know that more than one billion Uber rides have been completed – so we're talking about a lot of data. For those who use Uber on a regular basis, the company has a very detailed picture of your everyday life: where you live and work, where you travel, where you like to go for dinner, and when you like to do these things. Uber has recently partnered with Starwood Hotels and Resorts, launching a service that allows customers to connect their Starwood Preferred Guest Account. Customers get extra Starwood points when they take an Uber ride and, in return, Starwood gets access to all your Uber activity data. Clearly there is potential to roll out similar programmes with other hotel chains, airlines, even restaurants and bars.

Obviously, when you are trading in data, user permissions and data security become critical factors, and that's something I discuss more in Chapter 10. It is worth stating here though that users are generally happy for companies to use and profit from their data, providing the company has been transparent about what they're doing, and providing the user gets something in return. Uber is a great example of this, giving customers the opportunity to earn extra points by sharing their data with Starwood. I'm happy, even as a big data expert, to trade my data in return for an improved product or service, or extra convenience. I wear a fitness band, and I accept there's a trade-off between me having all this helpful data about my physical and sleep activity, and the manufacturer, Jawbone, being able to use that data for commercial purposes. I'm happy for the company to use my (anonymized) data, because I'm getting something in return, namely that their product makes it easier for me to lead a healthier lifestyle.

Likewise, in 2015, security firm AVG told *WIRED* magazine that, in order to offer free security software, the company might start to sell anonymized search and browser history data to advertisers and other companies – or, as they put it, 'employ a variety of means, including subscription, ads and data models'. Given that AVG provides the third most popular antivirus product in the world, we're talking about a lot of search and browser data. Reaction to the news was mixed but, on the whole, people seem happy to trade certain aspects of their data in return for a free, and very useful product.

Understanding the value of user-generated data

Many of the examples given in this chapter focus on user-generated or automatically generated data: think Facebook monitoring what you like and share, Uber tracking where you travel, Nest thermostats monitoring the conditions in your home, Amex tracking what you buy and where, etc. The really smart companies, those who are creating incredible value from data, are those with systems in place to collect or generate data automatically. In fact, Facebook users upload 2.5 million pieces of content every minute, giving Facebook a mountain of data for comparatively little effort.

I talk more about collecting data in the next chapter, but the key takeaway for now is that when data is automatically generated, or is generated by the company's users, this requires minimal effort by the company. Data that requires an expensive army of staff to collect and manage it, with all the costs that it entails, is unlikely to significantly boost value or revenue in real terms. Many data-based companies have surprisingly few employees, compared to other big companies of a similar value – they don't need them, because the mechanisms to collect and analyse data are so sophisticated, relatively little human interaction is required. Circling back to the top companies in the Fortune 500, four of the top five companies are data companies. Facebook, in fifth place, employs fewer than 13,000 people, while Exxon Mobil, in fourth place (and the only non-tech company in the top five) employs over 70,000 people.

Let's explore this notion in more detail by comparing Kodak with Instagram – two household names, one that pre-dates the digital age and one that is rooted in digital and data. Considering Instagram, the photo-sharing app, was bought by Facebook in 2012 for US $1 billion, you might be surprised to know the company had just 13 employees at the time of the sale. Instagram could run a very lean operation because their data systems were so good, they didn't need a lot of people working behind the scenes. Kodak, in contrast, had 145,000 employees at its peak, and still employs 8,000 people today. And Kodak's highest market value was less than Instagram's, peaking at around US $30 billion, while Instagram is valued at around $35 billion.

Instagram is another company based entirely around user-generated data. Its 400 million users spend an average of 20 minutes a day on the platform and upload 60 million photos a day – and this user-generated data is used by advertisers to target the site's primarily younger demographic. Indeed, Instagram expects to deliver a billion ad impressions per month in 2016, and ad revenue is projected to hit US $2.8 billion in 2017 (which will amount to 10 per cent of Facebook's total ad revenue). This is all particularly impressive when you consider Instagram was generating no revenue at all at the time of its 2012 sale. Facebook's purchase of Instagram may have raised eyebrows at the time, but they clearly had their eye on the long-term value of Instagram's user-generated data. Quite right they were too.

Sourcing and collecting data

06

Having identified what you are looking to achieve with data, you can now start to think about sourcing and collecting the best data to meet those needs. For example, if you are using data to improve your decision making, and you identified your key business questions as set out in Chapter 3, you now need to gather the data that will help you answer those questions. We've seen lots of examples so far of how various companies collect data, from Rolls-Royce collecting sensor data from their jet engines, to Amazon tracking what items customers browse, to Dickey's Barbecue Pit monitoring performance, sales and stock in their restaurants. There are many ways to source and collect data, including accessing or purchasing external data, using internal data and putting in place new collection methods. I explore each of these methods later in the chapter. Remember that the really smart companies put systems in place to collect or generate data automatically, whether it is data generated by users of a product or machine data from the manufacturing line. This is a clever way of collecting data with minimal effort (beyond setting up and maintaining the systems and processes).

It is also important to remember that no one type of data is inherently better than any other kind. Using data strategically is about finding the best data for you, and that may be very different to what's best for another company. With so much data available these days, the trick is to focus on finding the exact, specific pieces of data that will best benefit your organization. So, from a data strategy point of view, you need to describe the ideal data sets that would help you achieve your strategic objectives. You can then choose the best options for you based on how well they help you achieve your objectives, how easy it is to access or gather that data, and how cost effective it is.

I look at the different types of data in the next section but, generally speaking, internal structured data is the easiest to find and analyse, and usually the least expensive to acquire. At the other end of the scale, external and unstructured data is often more costly to acquire and more difficult (and therefore more expensive) to work with. You may find that you need more than one data set – in fact, it is often better to work with more than one data set to get a fuller picture. In my experience, it is often the combination of internal and external data that provides the most valuable insights. To meet your strategic goals, you may well need some structured internal data (like sales data), plus some structured external data (eg demographic data), alongside some unstructured internal data (such as customer feedback) and unstructured external data (eg social media analysis). The ideal strategic approach to sourcing data is to find the best combination of data to get the most useful insights for your business.

Once you know what data you need, your next step is to identify how you will collect or access it. Data collection tools include sensors, video, GPS, phone signals, social media platforms, and many more. The right tools for you will depend on your strategic objectives, but I explore some of the main options for accessing external data and collecting internal data later in the chapter. You also need to consider when you will collect the data. Is it something that needs to be collected very frequently? Is real-time data a must for your goals? There is no rule of thumb for when it's best to collect data; you will need to be guided by your strategic objectives.

Understanding the different types of data

Data collection in itself isn't new. Companies have had a lot of data for a long time (consider transactional records, HR files, mainframe computers, even early data centres). Until recently, though, the only data we could really work with was *structured* data, meaning it was typically housed in spreadsheets or databases, which made it easy to interrogate. But advances like the Internet, sensor technology, cloud computing, and our ability to store and analyse data have changed the type and quantity of data we can collect. Now, everyday activities like walking down the street, getting in the car, or buying something in a shop increasingly generate a huge trail of data, both structured and unstructured, and these many different types of data can all be used by companies to improve the way they do business.

Defining 'big data'

Big data is commonly understood through four main factors: volume, velocity, variety and veracity.[1] Therefore, for data to be classed as 'big data' it must satisfy at least one of these four Vs. Ultimately, it doesn't matter whether the data you're working with is 'big' or not – what matters is whether it can help your business succeed. However, because these four Vs define what is really special about big data, why it's so transformative, and just how far we've come in terms of working with data, it is worth spending a bit of time exploring each V.

- **Volume** refers to the vast amounts of data generated every second. We're no longer talking about good-old-fashioned gigabytes of data, but petabytes and even zettabytes or brontobytes of data. Data on this scale is simply too large to store in traditional ways, like on a mainframe computer, and it is too large to analyse using traditional database technology.

- **Velocity** refers to the speed at which new data is generated and the speed at which data moves around. Think of a tweet going viral in seconds, or a credit card company monitoring thousands of transactions in real time to spot fraudulent activity. While we used to have to store data and analyse it at a later date, now we have the technology to analyse data on the fly, as it's being generated, without ever putting it into databases. This is typical of the way many companies use data today.

- **Variety** refers to the different types of data we can now work with. In the past, we focused on structured data that neatly fitted into tables or databases, but now the vast majority of the world's data is unstructured (like photos or Facebook status updates), and can't easily be put into tables. Big data technology allows us to harness different types of data, including e-mails, social media conversations, photos, sensor data, video data and voice recordings, and bring them together with more traditional, structured data. For me, variety is the most interesting and exciting aspect of big data as it gives us the ability to extract more business-critical insights than ever before.

- **Veracity** refers to the messiness or trustworthiness of the data. Because we used to only be able to analyse neat and orderly structured data, we generally trusted that data as accurate. But now we can cope with completely unruly and unreliable data, like abbreviations, typos, slang, Twitter posts with incorrect hashtags, you name it. In many cases, the technology is there to cope with inaccuracies in the data. In some cases, these inaccuracies even provide an advantage – like Google using typos in web searches to enhance its predictive text capabilities.

I'd argue there's a fifth V of big data: **Value**. Because being able to work with vast volumes and many different varieties of data is all useless if it doesn't lead to any real business value. So, while the ever-increasing volume, velocity and variety of big data is all very exciting stuff, when it comes to business, value is clearly the most important V.

Defining structured data

Structured data is any data or information that is located in a fixed field within a defined record or file, usually in databases or spreadsheets. Essentially, it is data that is organized in a predetermined way, usually in rows and columns. Structured data is commonly managed using Structured Query Language (SQL) – a programming language dating back to the 1970s which is used for querying data in relational database management systems.

The average business has the potential to tap into a vast amount of structured data. The most common examples include customer data, sales data, transactional records, financial data, number of website visits, and any kind of machinery data points (eg temperature logs in a refrigerated storage facility). In fact, for now at least, structured data provides most of our current business insights – although that is changing.

Compared to the exciting world of unstructured data (which we'll get to next), structured data often gets a bad rap. I can see why. Despite being (for now) the most commonly used type of data, structured data represents just 20 per cent of all the data available in the world. The remaining 80 per cent of data out there is unstructured in format. Therefore, if you make use of structured data alone, you're potentially missing out on a lot of data. Another downside is that structured data is simply less rich in insights than unstructured data, which means it can present a very limited picture of what's going on. Therefore, often you need to use other data sources alongside structured data to gain better insights. For example, structured data will tell you that hits on your website decreased 25 per cent last month, but you'll need other forms of data to explore why that happened.

On the upside, structured data has some big advantages: it's usually cheap to use, it's easy to store, and it's easy to analyse. Despite its fixed nature, structured data can be queried and used in lots of different ways, often by non-analysts. And it can still be incredibly powerful and impressive. Walmart's transactional and customer databases, for example, contain more than 2.5 petabytes of data. (To put that in perspective, it's estimated that if we took all the content from all US academic research libraries, it would add up to just 2 petabytes.) The company is able to combine this structured customer data (particularly who bought what, when) with a variety of sources (like internal stock control records) to create sales promotions that are tailored to individual customers.

Even if you don't have 2.5 petabytes of structured data like Walmart (most companies don't), your own structured data can still serve as an excellent starting point for gathering insights. That's why I think it's a mistake to ignore structured data altogether. It still has plenty to offer businesses – particularly when it's combined with unstructured data.

Defining unstructured and semi-structured data

Unstructured data is the term for any data that doesn't fit neatly into traditional structured formats or databases. Examples include e-mail conversations, website text, social media posts, video content, photos, and audio recordings. As you can tell, it's often text-heavy, but may also contain data such as dates and numbers, or other types of data such as images. Up until relatively recently, everything that didn't fit into databases or spreadsheets was usually either discarded or stored on paper or microfiche or scanned files that could not be easily analysed. Now, thanks to massive increases in storage capabilities and the ability to tag and categorize unstructured data, not to mention advances in analytical tools (more on that in Chapter 7), we can finally make use of this data.

Semi-structured data is a cross between unstructured and structured data. This is data that may have some structure that can be used for analysis (like tags or other types of markers) but lacks the strict structure found in databases or spreadsheets. For example, a tweet can be categorized by author, date, time, length and even the sentiment behind the tweet, but the content itself is generally unstructured. It is possible, these days, to automatically analyse the text in that tweet, but not using traditional analytical methods – I would need a specialist text analysis tool.

You might guess from this that the main downside of working with messy, unstructured data is that it's complex stuff, usually requiring specially designed software and systems. As a result, the costs can add up. This is not unreasonable; unstructured data tends to be much bigger than structured data, which means you need bigger and better storage, and it's trickier to organize and extract insights from, which leads to the specialist systems. All this shouldn't put you off using unstructured data. It just means it's important to be very clear about what you're aiming to achieve and what data you need in order to do that – that's the surest way to avoid 'mission creep' and keep costs under control.

The big advantage of unstructured and semi-structured data is that there is so much of it. Eighty per cent of business-relevant data originates in unstructured or semi-structured data, so it massively outweighs structured data in terms of sheer volume. And another crucial advantage is that it tends to provide a richer picture than traditional structured data. Think of it as structured data telling you the *who*, *what*, *where* and *when*, while unstructured data helps you understand the *why*.

Here's a simple example of how we can now work with unstructured data more easily. Consider a video of a cat playing with a ball of string. A few years ago, for that video to be categorized (for example, so it would come up in search results), someone would have to watch it and tag it according to certain terms (cat, cute, ball, funny, etc) so that people searching for funny or cute cat videos could find it more easily. Now, videos can be automatically categorized using algorithms, meaning a computer can watch the video, automatically detect what's in it (maybe even who is in it, thanks to facial recognition software), and produce its own tags automatically. Brands are starting to use this technology as part of their everyday marketing activities. A friend of mine runs conferences for a living, and one of the conferences he ran was for a well-known electronics manufacturer. Just before the conference started, he shared a picture on Twitter of the main stage, ready for the first speaker. The picture featured the manufacturer's name and logo, which was on a sign behind the stage, but he didn't mention the company explicitly using a hashtag or their Twitter handle. So why, the week after the conference, did he keep seeing targeted ads online for that particular brand? Because the company knew he was talking about them; their analytical software was able to mine unstructured data like social media posts and photos for anything related to their company and their products.

Defining internal data

Internal data refers to all the information your business currently has or has the potential to collect. Internal data can be structured in format (like a customer database or transactional records) or it could be unstructured (like conversational data from customer service calls or feedback from employee interviews). It is your private or proprietary data that is owned by your business – and this means that only your company controls access to the data. There are many, many types of internal data but some of the most common examples include customer and employee survey data, conversational data from your customer services calls, sales data, financial data, HR data, customer records, stock control data, CCTV video data, sensor data from company machines or vehicles, and your own website data (like number of visitors, etc).

One downside to internal data is the fact that you are responsible for maintaining and securing that data. It costs money to properly maintain and secure data, particularly personal data, around which there are strict legal requirements, whereas when you buy in external data, the data supplier has taken on that responsibility and liability for you. Another disadvantage is that internal data on its own may not provide enough information to meet your strategic goals, and you may need to supplement it with external data. Rather like blending structured and unstructured data to get a really rich picture of what's going on, often it is necessary to combine internal data with external data to get the most useful insights.

On the upside, internal data is usually cheap or free to access, which often makes it a good starting point when considering your data options. Plus, as you own the data, there are no access issues to deal with. You're never at the whim of a third party that can jack up prices or cut off access at any time. For really business-critical information, issues around access and ownership should not be taken lightly. Finally, there's real value in your internal data because it's already tailored to your business or industry. So, while you may need to look at some external data alongside your internal data to get the best results, you should never overlook it altogether.

Like structured data, internal data isn't seen as particularly exciting or innovative, but it can provide a wealth of information. One brilliant example comes from the streaming service Netflix. In recent years, Netflix have moved towards positioning themselves as a content creator, not just a distribution method for movie studios and other networks. Their strategy here has been firmly driven by their internal data – which showed that Netflix subscribers had a voracious appetite for content directed by David Fincher and starring Kevin Spacey. Based on this, after outbidding networks including HBO and ABC for the rights to *House of Cards*, they were so confident the show fitted their predictive model for the 'perfect TV show' that they bucked the convention of producing a pilot and immediately commissioned the first two seasons. Netflix's ability to mine their in-house data for valuable viewer insights has really paid off. The service added a record 5.59 million new subscribers in the fourth quarter of 2015 alone, and Netflix have put much of this success down to their 'ever-improving content', like *House of Cards* and *Orange Is the New Black*. In this way, insights from Netflix's internal data are helping to drive new member acquisition and customer retention.

Defining external data

External data is the infinite array of information that exists outside of your organization. This can be publicly available (like certain government data) or privately owned by a third party (like Amazon), and it can also be structured or unstructured in format. Key examples of external data include social media data, Google Trends data, government census data, economic data, and weather data. There are plenty of ready-made data sets, both public and private, that are available to suit a range of needs (census data being a good example). However, you may need a more bespoke data set. If that's the case, you can pay a third-party provider to provide or gather the data for you.

The obvious downside to external data is that you don't own the data and you will often have to pay for access (not always, but often). This also means you are reliant on an external source, which can be risky if the data is absolutely critical to your key business functions. You will need to weigh up the risks and the costs of accessing external data against the risks and costs of not using that data. Would you have to go to the trouble of creating it yourself? Would your business suffer if you didn't use that data? Would it stop you meeting your strategic goals? You may find that, overall, the benefits far outweigh the risks.

There are some significant advantages to external data, though. Companies like Walmart and Amazon have the capabilities, infrastructure and budget to generate and manage huge amounts of data themselves. That's great for them. But many businesses can never dream of having that much data at their disposal. External data gives any business the capability to access and mine data for insights – without many of the hassles that come with storing, managing and securing that data on a daily basis. For smaller businesses, this can be a significant advantage. Plus, external data is often richer and more complex (and possibly even more up to date) than anything you could generate in-house.

Here's an example of a company successfully harnessing external data from a variety of sources. California-based cognitive computing firm Apixio was founded in 2009 with the vision of uncovering and making accessible clinical knowledge from digitized medical records, in order to improve healthcare decision making. Traditional evidence-based medicine is largely based upon studies with methodological flaws, or randomized clinical trials with relatively small populations that may not generalize well outside that particular study. But, by mining the vast amounts of real-life, practice-based clinical data – who has what condition, what treatments are working, etc – healthcare providers can learn a lot about the way they care for individuals and how care can be improved. To make this a reality, Apixio devised a way to access and make sense of clinical information from a variety of sources. Electronic health records (EHRs) have been around for a while, but they are not designed to facilitate data analysis and contain data stored across a number of different systems and formats. So, before Apixio can even analyse any data, they first have to extract the data from these various sources (which may include doctors' notes, hospital records, government Medicare records, etc). This array of data can be analysed at an individual level to create a detailed patient data model, thereby helping clinicians make better treatment decisions and provide more individualized care. But it can also be aggregated across the population in order to derive larger insights around disease prevalence, treatment patterns, etc.

Taking a look at newer types of data

The fact that we're leaving more and more digital traces than ever before creates many new types of data for companies to work with. Some of the data we can now collect is new (like biometric data from an Apple Watch), while some has been around for ages but we've only recently found ways to really analyse it (conversation data from customer service calls, for instance). Therefore, I wanted to spend a bit of time highlighting the many new types of data that companies have at their disposal: activity data, conversation data, photo and video data, and sensor data. It's important to be clear that all of these are still either structured, unstructured or semi-structured types of data. I have simply grouped them together here because they represent some of the biggest business-related leaps in data and analytics – which makes them useful considerations for any data strategy.

Activity data

This is the computer record of human actions or activities that occur online or in the offline physical world. If I think about everything I have done today before sitting down to write this chapter, most of those activities have left some digital trace that can be (and probably is being) collected and analysed. My phone calls create data and, depending on who I speak to (for example, if it's my bank or a customer service department), the actual content of that call may be recorded and analysed. Buying my wife a birthday present creates transaction data. Even browsing online for gift ideas creates a whole trail of data, including where I accessed the Internet from, what sites I visited, how I moved around those sites, what products held my attention and how long I spent on the sites. Everything I like on Facebook or share on LinkedIn or Twitter creates a trail. Even if I choose to switch off my phone and laptop and go for a run, my fitness band tracks my movements, how far I travel and how many calories I burned. Local CCTV cameras would also pick up my image along my favourite route.

As you might imagine, the sheer volume of activity data available can make it difficult to pinpoint exactly what to collect. Continually circling back to your strategic objectives will help you concentrate on the best activity data for you, but it is hard not to get swept up in the many tempting possibilities that activity data presents. Another disadvantage is that the majority of activity data is unstructured, which can make it more difficult and expensive to work with.

On the positive side, activity data allows you to see what your customers actually do, as opposed to what they say they do or what you assume they do, which can be vital information for product or service development. And, because we're creating more and more data every day, with practically every activity, there is an almost endless supply of rich data to tap into. Best of all, activity data is usually self-generating, which minimizes the amount of work for your business.

Conversation data

This doesn't just apply to an out-loud conversation with someone on the end of the phone. Conversation data also covers any conversation you may have in any format, from an SMS message or instant message through your phone, to e-mails, blog comments, social media posts, and more. It's all conversation data.

Conversation data can be extremely useful for businesses because it provides insights into how happy or otherwise your customers, clients, employees and suppliers are. Conversations can be mined for content (what is said) as well as context (how it's said). In other words, you can understand what is going on from the words used and the mood of the person engaged in the conversation. This means companies can now figure out how angry or irritated a customer or employee is, or even if they are telling the truth about something, just from the stress levels in that person's voice.

Obviously, if you are planning to record any conversation, you need to be aware of any legal ramifications in your country. Generally speaking, you can't record customers or employees just because you feel like it; what you're recording must be relevant to the business. Also, you need to inform the parties that they are being recorded so that they can opt out. In addition, keep in mind that conversation data is also unstructured, which can make it more difficult and expensive to analyse.

On the plus side, conversation data gives you real-time access to customers and an accurate insight into what those customers really think and feel about your brand, product and services. It's a very powerful tool if you're looking to improve the service you provide.

Photo and video data

Our ever-increasing attachment to our smartphones, and the commonplace use of CCTV cameras (particularly in the UK), has resulted in an explosion of photo and video image data. In days gone by, companies may have recorded their retail or storage premises for security purposes, but the recordings were never stored long-term. The recording was made to tape and then after a week or so the tape would be used again and new recordings would be made over the old ones. Now, some of the more data-savvy stores are keeping all the CCTV camera footage and analysing it to study how people walk through the shops, where they stop, what they look at and for how long so they can make alterations to offers and boost sales. Some are even using facial recognition software to pinpoint individual customers.

Photo and video data can create huge files, which can be tricky to store and manage. It's therefore important to make sure you have a defined and relevant business need for collecting and storing this type of data. However, if you're already collecting this data as a matter of routine (perhaps through security footage), finding better ways to use it may not be very expensive at all.

Sensor data

As we've seen throughout the book, a vast amount of data is being generated and transmitted from sensors that are increasingly being built into products. Your smartphone alone contains a GPS sensor, an accelerometer sensor (which measures how quickly the phone is moving), a gyroscope (which measures orientation and rotates the screen), a proximity sensor (which measures how close you are to other people, locations or objects), an ambient sensor (for adjusting the backlight on your phone), and a Near Field Communication sensor (this is what allows you to make a payment by waving your phone over a payment machine).

Sensor data often lacks context and only measures a very small part of reality, which means it most likely needs to be combined with another data set to get the best results. However, on the plus side, sensor data is self-generating, which makes it very appealing indeed. And many devices, such as smartphones, contain ready-to-use sensors that can be used to your advantage (think of a delivery company using sensors in their drivers' phones to track delivery routes). Sensor data can also provide very powerful insights for improving productivity and maintenance.

Gathering your internal data

Having identified the data you need, it makes sense to see if you're already sitting on some of that information, even if it isn't immediately obvious. Consider whether the data you need already exists internally, or whether you have the capability to generate it yourselves, ie by collecting data from your systems, products, customers or employees. Nowadays, you can gather data from any of your apps, software, or indeed any digital process – meaning almost any aspect of running a business can be monitored and analysed.

Wherever you are currently having conversations, there is an opportunity to collect conversation data. If you operate a telephone sales department or customer service department where customers call in to purchase or follow up on order delivery, then you could record those conversations and analyse the content and sentiment for useful insights. Text-based conversation data also exists in internal documents and e-mails, and the e-mails you receive from your customers.

You can create your own data by asking questions and capturing the answers, through surveys, focus groups, asking people to rate your products, or by capturing details when customers register for something. You also can run experiments to gather data, for example, by running a marketing campaign, observing the results, and tweaking parameters if necessary to find different insights.

Video and photo data can be obtained by simply starting to collect it using digital cameras. You may already be using video for security purposes, in which case you may be able to use those for analysis. For example, retailers can use their network of CCTV cameras to analyse how customers walk through the shop, where they stop and which parts they ignore. Testing the existing data shows up any gaps where new cameras or systems will have to be added to improve the analysis.

Transaction data provides another mine of information for companies, and it usually very easy to access and analyse. It shows you what your customers bought and when. Depending on what you measure, it can also show where the item was purchased, how the customer came across the product and whether they took advantage of a promotion. Even basic transaction records can be very useful for measuring sales, monitoring stock levels and predicting what you need to order (or manufacture). In fact, all your company's financial data, not just the transactions, should be considered. Finance data has many uses such as predicting cash flow and influencing investment and other long-term business decisions. It can be especially powerful when combined with other kinds of data. For example, you might look at your own internal financial data along with external data about industry trends and the wider economy.

Crucially, you can build the ability to collect data into every aspect of a product or service, whether you make tractors or washing machines or sell insurance. Sensor data is particularly helpful in this respect, and, these days, sensors can be incorporated into almost anything – from manufacturing equipment to shop doors to tennis racquets. Sensors are tiny, affordable, and very easy to add to products. They are revolutionizing the way businesses interact with their customers, enabling them to understand how customers actually use their products and to make personal recommendations. Swedish car manufacturer Volvo, for example, is using data to improve driver and passenger convenience and create a more user-friendly product. Volvo monitors the use of applications and comfort features to see what their customers are finding useful, and what is being underused or ignored. This includes entertainment features like built-in connectivity with streaming media services, as well as practical tools such as GPS, traffic incident reporting, parking space location and weather information.

It's clear that internal data can be a gold mine, and is an essential part of any good data strategy. Even if you need to combine your internal data with some external data to get a fuller picture, the data you already have (or have the potential to capture) is so unique to your business, it should never be overlooked.

Accessing external data

As well as your internal data, you can make use of external data that is already out there. As more and more companies view data as a business commodity, a market is emerging where practically any organization can buy, sell and trade data. (Indeed, many companies exist purely to supply other companies with data.) Experian is one example of a company selling valuable data, as well as other big players like Amazon and IBM. But there are also lots of smaller, more industry-focused data providers. So even if you need quite specialized data, there's a good chance someone else is already gathering it. In addition, a lot of valuable data is being collected and shared by open government data initiatives, scientific research organizations, and other not-for-profit agencies. Most governments these days make concerted efforts to make as much of their data as possible available free of charge. This can be a great source of information on everything from population to weather and crime statistics.

Clearly social media platforms are critical sources of data, and they provide a wealth of information on customers. You can, for example, use sentiment analysis to find out what your customers are saying about your product or service online. Facebook is likely to be your first stop for social media big data. Facebook data encompasses text data, photo data, video data, and user 'likes'. All this data can be analysed and used to your business's advantage – whether you want to target a promotion or understand how many pregnant women live in a certain area. Facebook offers incredibly useful breakdowns of customer information and analyses of all the data they have. (Some of this you will need to purchase, but plenty is available for free.) Although some of the information on users' Facebook profiles is private (depending on how savvy they are with their settings), a lot of it is not. Facebook has developed the Graph API (Application Program Interface) as a way of querying the huge amount of information that its users share with the world. Even if a user has their privacy settings cranked up to the highest level (which many people don't bother to do), Facebook can still provide information to companies about what they're saying – just not *who* specifically is saying it.

Twitter is another excellent source of data. Every time a Twitter user mentions a company or product, it is visible to everyone, including the company. Even if a product isn't mentioned explicitly in the text of the tweet, companies can detect if their product features in a photo. Examples of this might include a drinks company finding pictures of people drinking their product, restaurants finding pictures taken in their restaurant, or fashion houses finding out who is wearing their clothes. You can also use sentiment analysis on Twitter posts to gain insights into the popularity of a product or service, understand customer satisfaction, and deal with any problems swiftly. Sentiment analysis can tell us a lot about users' feelings, opinions and experiences, without having to trawl through individual tweets one at a time. In one example of Twitter sentiment analysis, researchers were able to predict which women were most at risk of developing postnatal depression. They analysed Twitter posts, searching for verbal clues in the weeks leading up to the birth. They found that negative language and words hinting at unhappiness, as well as an increased use of the word 'I', indicated an increased chance of developing postnatal depression.

Google Trends is a very powerful and versatile tool, providing statistics on search volume (as a proportion of total searches) for any given term since 2004. You can see search popularity for certain phrases or words and how it has changed over time, and you can narrow the results by your geographic location. This is helpful for understanding trends in your industry, what is popular right now, and what is becoming more popular (or less popular). It's a great way of gauging consumer interest.

Government data sets can also be very valuable. In 2013, the US government pledged to make all government data available freely online through its data.gov site, and the site is an absolute treasure trove of information. It acts as a portal to all sorts of government data on everything from climate to crime rates. You can use it for research purposes or it can serve as a useful tool for developing web and mobile applications. Data.gov.uk is the UK equivalent.

Census data is a very useful source of population data, geographic data and education data. Demographic data like this can be a useful indicator of trends, which is especially helpful if you're developing a new product or service. It can also help you target products or services to particular local demographics.

Weather data, like that available through the US National Climatic Data Centre or the UK's Met Office, can be used in a number of ways, from estimating customer numbers and planning staffing levels, to deciding how much ice cream to stock on a given weekend.

There are thousands upon thousands of options for accessing external sources of data, and the options are growing every day. In this way, many organizations will find that the data they need already exists – or much of it already exists, greatly reducing what they specifically need to collect and store internally. Keep in mind, though, that you're looking for the right data for you, ie the data that best helps you achieve your strategic goals. If a provider's data doesn't help you do that, then it doesn't matter how big or impressive their data set is, it's not the right one for you.

When the data you want doesn't exist

When the best data for you doesn't already exist, you have to find ways to generate and collect it. In many sectors and industries, businesses are fighting to be the first to collect new data and turn that data into value. Often there is a distinct competitive advantage in being the first company to collect data.

One agricultural data company, Springg, has come up with a way of collecting and analysing data on the fly – data that wasn't previously available in developing countries. The company recognized that farmers in developing nations could benefit from the same data as that available to farmers in developed nations, such as soil quality data. But in rural and underdeveloped areas, the practice of taking a soil sample and then sending it off to a lab for analysis can take weeks, which can dramatically and negatively impact the farmer's current season of crops. As a result, there wasn't really any data available to work with because no one was bothering to gather it. So Springg developed mobile test centres with IoT devices that could test the soil remotely, give results almost immediately, and then send the data back to a central repository for further analysis alongside all the other soil samples. Obviously, this information benefits the farmers involved, but it's also a big win for Springg, who have collected aggregated data on soil conditions from places where it has never been done before. And because this information could be of real value to the commodities markets and other businesses, Springg could reap significant benefits from being first to market with the data. Finding innovative ways of collecting new data like this helps companies get this valuable first-mover advantage. This is true in more or less any area of data and analytics. Weather companies, for example, are constantly fighting for the latest ways of collecting data.

This sort of bespoke data collection requires a sophisticated network of devices and technologies to collect the data, possibly including wireless networks, smartphones, IoT sensors, and flexible communications protocols. But the competitive and financial advantages can be significant. Companies with the foresight and creativity to build the infrastructure (physical and technical) required to collect, analyse and use never-before-used data will be rewarded with all the rights and benefits that come with collecting and 'discovering' it.

Endnote

1 As early as 2001, META Group (now Gartner) analyst Doug Laney defined data growth challenges across three dimensions: increasing volume, velocity and variety. These dimensions have later been expanded by others, including IBM, who capture the four Vs well in this infographic: http://www.ibmbigdatahub. com/infographic/four-vs-big-data

Turning data into insights

07

Having identified the ideal data for your business, your next step is to identify how to turn that data into useful insights and applications. Analytics is the process of collecting, processing and analysing data to generate insights that help you improve the way you do business. In most cases, it involves software-based analysis using algorithms. By analysing data with algorithms and analytic tools, you can extract the insights you need to answer your key business questions, improve operational performance, monetize data, and meet your strategic goals. Data and analytics are like two sides of the same coin. After all, what's the point of having all this business data and capturing new and exciting types of data if we don't do anything with it? Analytics allows us to learn new things, understand more about the world in which we operate, and make improvements across the organization. In this way, it is analytics that provides the fifth V of big data: value.

Therefore, as part of any solid data strategy, you will need to plan how you will apply analytics to your data. This will, in turn, affect the data infrastructure and competencies that need to be put in place (more on those in Chapters 8 and 9). What analytics you apply will depend on your strategic objectives. And, just as with collecting data, it is important to understand what's possible with analytics before you can decide the best option for your business. Therefore, in this chapter, I look at how analytics has evolved over the years and identify some of the key analytic approaches that businesses are using today.

Keep in mind, though, that it is very easy to get caught up in the exciting opportunities that analytics brings. Organizations are doing very cool things with analytics, but what works for one business may not work for yours. The challenge in creating a robust data strategy is to identify the best, most accessible, most achievable analytic approach for you. Having said that, advances in analytics, AI and machine learning are moving so fast that it is safe to assume that new and improved ways of extracting value from data will emerge very, very soon. Therefore, while it's important to understand what is currently available and possible with analytics, and identify what is best for your business right now, it is also worthwhile putting together a wish list of how you might like to analyse data in the future. It is not unreasonable to assume that some or all of the approaches on your wish list will become a reality in the near future.

How analytics has evolved

As we saw in Chapter 6, it's clear that we're in the middle of a data explosion. The ever-increasing volume and variety of data are, in turn, fuelling huge leaps in analytic technology. In the past, when we wanted to collect data and analyse it to understand what the data was telling us, that data needed to be contained in a structured database and we could only use SQL tools to interrogate the data. It sounds basic but, in fact, it worked very well. Using databases and SQL analysis, businesses could manage stock levels, keep track of orders, log customer information, and understand how their sales and revenue were shaping up. Using database technology, it's easy even for a non-analyst to understand how many units of product X you sold in November last year, and you can use this to inform your stock decisions for this Christmas. You can also understand what you sold, when, to whom and for how much. Businesses have therefore been working with structured data in this way for decades. But, for unstructured data – data which doesn't fit neatly into a database or spreadsheet – it was pretty much impossible (or very expensive and time consuming) to analyse that data for insights. Now, we no longer need database technology or structure to gain insights from data. Advances in analytic technology have made it possible to work with just about any kind of data, whether it is structured, unstructured, in a spreadsheet, on Facebook, or contained in a security video.

We're generating more data than ever before – as we saw in Chapter 1, every two days we create as much data as we did from the beginning of time until 2003. Naturally, this gives us more data to work with and more opportunities to extract business-critical insights. Every day we generate 4.5 billion Facebook likes and 500 million tweets – that's data that wasn't being generated at all 12 years ago, and on a vastly smaller scale even five years ago. All this data provides an unprecedented opportunity for companies to understand the world in which they operate, from what their customers really think and do, to who is likely to buy what and when, to how to get the most out of machines and processes.

Cloud computing has had a lot to do with these leaps in analytic technology, and the two are closely linked. Cloud computing gives us massively increased storage capability and computing power. Without this, we wouldn't be able to store and analyse the wide variety and huge volume of data that is possible today. Thanks to increased storage and computing power, we can now analyse large volumes of fast-moving data from different data sources, even in real time, to gain insights that were never possible before. Storage systems like Hadoop (which I cover in Chapter 8) make it possible for businesses to store and analyse data sets far larger than can practically be stored and accessed on one storage device (such as a hard disk). Distributed computing means the analysis of large amounts of data can be spread across many different computers, with each computer taking on a small chunk of the overall analytic load. By breaking up the analysis this way, it can be done in a faster and more efficient way – and it's much more cost effective too.

Looking at the different types of analytics

There are many tools and techniques for analysing data, including text analytics, video analytics and sentiment analysis. In the last few years, lots of new analytics tools have come onto the market, greatly improving our ability to analyse data. There are new companies springing up every week that offer businesses the ability to analyse data in one way or another. But with so many options available, it can be difficult to know what to use and when. Here I take a look at some of the key analytic tools that businesses are using today and when they are particularly useful. In almost all cases, there are many commercially available tools on the market that simplify these analytic processes.

Text analytics

Also known as text mining, text analytics is a process of extracting value from large quantities of unstructured text data. Most businesses have a huge amount of text-based data from memos, company documents, e-mails, reports, press releases, customer records and communication, websites, blogs and social media posts. Until recently, however, it wasn't always that useful. While the text is structured to make sense to a human being, it is unstructured from an analytics perspective because it doesn't fit neatly into a relational database or rows and columns of a spreadsheet. Access to huge text data sets and improved technical capability means text can be analysed to extract additional high-quality information above and beyond what the document actually says. For example, text can be assessed for commercially relevant patterns such as an increase or decrease in positive feedback from customers, or patterns that could lead to product or service improvements.

Some of the ways we can now analyse text include:

- Text categorization – applying some structure to a text so that it can be classified by features such as author, subject, date, etc.

- Text clustering – grouping text into topics or categories to make filtering easier. Search engines use this technology all the time.

- Concept extraction – honing in on the text that is most relevant to the task at hand.

- Sentiment assessment – extracting opinion or sentiment from text and categorizing it as positive, negative or neutral (more on this below).

- Document summarization – distilling documents down to the key points.

Text analytics helps us get more out of text, so that we can understand more than just the words on the page or screen. Therefore, it's especially helpful for understanding more about your customers. It can also be applied internally to analyse what your employees are saying. For example, I know one organization that uses text analytics tools to scan and analyse the content of e-mails sent by their staff as well as their social media posts. This allows them to accurately understand the levels of staff engagement, meaning they no longer need to carry out those expensive and time-consuming traditional staff surveys.

Sentiment analysis

Sentiment analysis, also known as opinion mining, seeks to extract subjective opinion or sentiment from text, video or audio data. The basic aim is to determine the attitude of an individual or group regarding a particular topic or overall context. The sentiment or attitude may be a judgement, evaluation or emotional reaction.

Use sentiment analysis when you want to understand stakeholder opinion. Sentiment analysis seeks to get to the real truth behind communication so that businesses can make better decisions by working out if stakeholders feel positively, negatively or neutrally about their products, business and brand. Advanced, 'beyond polarity' sentiment analysis can also go further by making a classification as to the emotional state involved. For example, text, audio tonality or facial expressions can determine whether the person is frustrated, angry, or happy. We have known for decades that the words we use to communicate and express ourselves only account for 7 per cent of comprehension. The vast majority of our communication is picked up non-verbally through body language and tonality, and this can now be analysed on a large scale. This type of analytics is becoming increasingly popular with the rise of social media, blogs and social networks where people are sharing their thoughts and feelings about all sorts of things – including companies and products – much more readily.

Image analytics

This is the process of extracting information, meaning and insights from images such as photographs, medical images or graphics. As a process, it relies heavily on pattern recognition, digital geometry and signal processing. In the past, the only analysis that was possible on images was via the human eye or, if computers were used, by assessing descriptor keywords (like 'cute' and 'cat') that were manually added to the image to help people find it. Now, image analytics is considerably more sophisticated. In the case of photographs, a digital photograph contains a lot more information than you might imagine, including when and where it was taken, based on GPS coordinates embedded in the photo. All those additional properties can be analysed to extract more information above and beyond the actual image content.

Image analytics can be used in a number of ways, such as facial recognition for security purposes or recognizing your brand or product in photographs shared on social media platforms. Casinos are currently using image analytics to identify high rollers for special treatment – and presumably to identify people they want to keep out of their casinos, too. Exciting as this technology is, remember that image analytics is only really going to be useful if it helps to answer key strategic questions or deliver your long-term goals.

Video analytics

Video analytics is the process of extracting information, meaning and insights from video footage. It includes everything that image analytics can do, plus it can also measure and track behaviour.

You could use video analytics if you wanted to increase security or understand more about who is visiting your store or premises and what they are doing when they get there. It is, for example, now possible to collect data from different CCTV cameras in a retail environment, upload that data to a cloud server without additional infrastructure requirements and analyse the footage to see how your customers behave and how they move through the store. This data can help you to see how many people stop at a particular product display or offer for example, how long they engage with it and whether or not it is converting into sales.

You could also use video analytics to reduce costs and risk and assist decision making. For example, there is now software that allows you to automatically monitor a location 24/7. That video footage is then analysed using a video and behavioural analytics solution which alerts you in real time to any abnormal and suspicious activity. Once installed and provided with the initial video feed, the software observes its environment, learns to distinguish normal behaviour from abnormal behaviour. The system is also self-correcting, which means that it continuously refines its own assumptions about behaviour and no human effort is required to define its parameters.

Voice analytics

Also known as speech analytics, voice analytics is the process of extracting information from audio recordings of conversations. This form of analytics can analyse the topics or actual words and phrases being used, as well as the emotional content of the conversation.

All businesses need to keep their customers happy if they want to stay in business and stay ahead of the competition. If you have a product or service that requires technical assistance, for example, or you have large customer service call centres, then this type of analytics can be really useful in maintaining and building ongoing customer relationships as well as highlighting issues that need to be addressed. You could, for example, use voice analytics to help identify recurring themes around customer complaints or recurring technical issues. These insights could help you to spot these potential pitfalls quicker and solve them before your customers take to social media to complain.

Voice analytics can also be used to help you identify when your customers are getting upset. By analysing the pitch and intonations of conversations taking place in your call centre, you can gauge the emotional state of your customers and intervene quickly when they are getting angry or frustrated. This type of analytics is also very useful in helping to identify under-performing customer service representatives so they can receive additional training or coaching.

Data mining

Data mining is often used as a buzzword or generic description applied to any form of large-scale information processing, but this is not very accurate. Data mining is in fact an analytic process designed to explore data, usually very large business-related data sets, looking for commercially relevant insights, patterns or relationships between variables that can improve performance. Data mining is essentially a hybrid of artificial intelligence, statistics, database systems, database research and machine learning. The actual process entails the automatic or semi-automatic analysis of large data sets to extract previously unknown yet interesting patterns, anomalies or dependencies that could be exploited.

There are three stages to this process: 1) initial exploration, 2) model building and validation, and 3) deployment.

The ultimate goal of data mining is prediction. Therefore, you would use data mining if you had large data sets and wanted to extract insights from that data that could help your business in the future. Clearly, in business, being able to predict the future is helpful and can not only reduce costs and assist with planning and strategy but insights gained from data mining could potentially change the direction of the business.

Insights extracted from data mining can also guide decision making and reduce risk. It's important to appreciate, though, that data mining may throw up patterns, anomalies or inter-dependencies but it will not necessarily tell you the reason for those patterns, anomalies or inter-dependencies. Additional analysis will be required if the 'why' is still important to you.

Business experiments

Business experiments, experimental design and A/B testing are all techniques for testing the validity of something, whether it's a strategic hypothesis, new product packaging or a marketing approach. It is basically about trying something in one part of the organization and then comparing it with another part where the changes were not made (used as a control group). Essentially business experimentation can help you to decide which option to get behind when you are faced with two or more choices. Whether you want to understand the possibility of brand damage or the financial and time cost to the business, running a test between the various options on a smaller, more manageable scale can allow you to work out which one is likely to yield the best results. Plus, the feedback from the experiments can help you to further refine and improve the winning option to make it even more effective.

The basic process for running business experiments, as outlined by analytics expert Thomas H Davenport, is: 1) create a hypothesis, 2) design the experiment, 3) run the experiment, and 4) analyse results and follow up. Probably the biggest advantage of business experimentation is that it allows you to test things without great expense or risk.

Visual analytics

Data can be analysed in different ways and the simplest way is to create a visual or graph and look at it to spot patterns and trends. This is an integrated approach that combines data analysis with data visualization and human interaction. It is especially useful when you are trying to make sense of a huge volume of data and/or if the complexity of the problem you face could be assisted by some additional computational horsepower.

Essentially, visual analytics can help you spot patterns and trends in data and allow you to make vast amounts of data accessible and understandable to anyone, even if they aren't a data scientist or statistician. It is therefore extremely useful for bridging the gap between the data and the insights, but only when you stick to what's really needed. Just because a visual analytics program can present and manipulate the data a thousand different ways doesn't mean you need to present and manipulate the data a thousand different ways! Stay focused on what needs to be answered.

Correlation analysis

This is a statistical technique that helps you determine whether there is a relationship between two separate variables and how strong that relationship may be. This type of analysis is only appropriate if the data is quantified and represented by a number. It can't be used for categorical data, such as gender, brands purchased, or colour. The analysis produces a single number between +1 and −1 that describes the degree of relationship between two variables. If the result is positive then the two variables are positively correlated to each other, ie when one is high, the other one tends to be high too. If the result is negative then the two variables are negatively correlated to each other, ie when one is high, the other one tends to be low.

You should use correlation analysis when you suspect that there is a relationship between two variables and you would like to test your assumption. For example, you may believe that temperature is affecting sales. Correlation analysis would allow you to work out whether that assumption is true. Alternatively, you can use correlation analysis when you want to know which of several pairs of variables shows the strongest correlation. So you may want to see whether temperature affects sales more than time of year, for example. And finally, you can use this type of analysis speculatively just to see what emerges. Sometimes correlation analysis will highlight an unexpected relationship that could warrant further analysis and potential exploitation. For example, Walmart discovered an unexpected relationship between the purchase of Pop-Tarts and a hurricane warning. Apparently, when there was a severe weather warning in the United States, the sale of Pop-Tarts increased. This knowledge allowed Walmart to position Pop-Tarts at the entrance of the store following a hurricane warning, further pushing up sales.

You can carry out correlation analysis with a manual calculation known as 'Pearson's correlation coefficient', or you can use one of the many correlation tools on the market which aim to simplify the process.

Regression analysis

Regression analysis is a statistical tool for investigating the relationship between variables, for example whether there is a causal relationship between price and product demand. Regression analysis is often talked about alongside correlation analysis and as such it's often quite difficult to know which is which and what the difference is. Essentially, regression analysis identifies the relationships between two variables and plots the course of that relationship, which can then be projected into the future. Correlation analysis, on the other hand, explores the *strength* of that relationship.

Use regression analysis if you believe that one variable is affecting another and you want to establish whether your hypothesis is true. You can also gauge the 'statistical significance' of the estimated relationships. In other words, you can work out how confident you can be that there is a close, and therefore predictable, relationship between the variables.

At the start of any regression analysis, you need to formulate a hypothesis about the relationship between the variables of interest. You may, for example, believe that the more educated someone is, the more money they will earn. The tentative hypothesis for this assertion could be, 'higher levels of educational attainment cause higher levels of earnings where all other things are equal'. You would then need to test this hypothesis using a regression model.

Scenario analysis

Scenario analysis, also known as horizon analysis or total return analysis, is an analytic process that allows you to analyse a variety of possible future events or scenarios by considering alternative possible outcomes. By planning out the detail required to implement a particular decision or course of action, you can observe not only the final potential outcome but the viability of the path leading to that outcome. Often it's only when you really consider what would be involved in the actual implementation of an idea that you fully appreciate the scope of that idea. Scenario analysis therefore allows you to improve decision making by fully considering the outcomes you expect and their implementation implications without the cost and time involved in actual real-world implementation. Scenario analysis does not rely on historical data and it doesn't expect the future to be the same as the past or seek to extrapolate the past into the future. Rather, it tries to consider possible future developments and turning points.

You should use scenario analysis when you are unsure which decision to take or which course of action to pursue. It can be especially useful if the implications of the decision are significant, for example if the decision would cost a great deal of time or money to implement or if the ramifications of getting the decision wrong could be fatal for the business. It can be used to assess the possible likely future of different strategic choices or to generate a combination of different scenarios that look at the same scenario but from three different perspectives: the optimistic version of events, the pessimistic version of events and the most likely scenario. It is also a very useful tool if you are unclear about what is going to be involved in the execution of a strategy or decision, as the process pushes you to really engage with the scenario you are testing. This enhanced engagement can help to anticipate more of the pros and cons of each scenario, thereby reducing risk and directing you to the best choice.

Scenario planning usually consists of a five-stage process: 1) define the problem, 2) gather the data, 3) separate certainties from uncertainties, 4) develop scenarios, and 5) use the outcome in your planning.

Forecasting/time series analysis

Time series data is data that is collected at uniformly spaced intervals, such as the closing value of the FTSE or the annual flow volume of the Thames. It is data that is measured consistently at particular times to plot the changes. Time series analysis explores this data to extract meaningful statistics or data characteristics. By analysing time series data, you can identify patterns that can then be extrapolated out into the future.

You can therefore use time series analysis when you want to assess changes over time or predict future events based on what has happened in the past. Time series data is usually plotted via a line chart and this type of analysis is frequently used in statistics, pattern recognition, mathematics, finance and weather forecasting, including severe weather or earthquake prediction. Two of the most common processes for conducting time series analysis are autoregressive process and moving average process. Both involve very complex equations, so you are probably better off investing in a commercial analytic tool.

Monte Carlo simulation

This is a mathematical problem-solving and risk-assessment technique that approximates the probability and the risk of certain outcomes using computerized simulations of random variables. In essence, this technique illustrates the extreme possibilities that could occur. By looking at the implications from worst-case scenario through the middle ground and into best-case scenario, along with the probability of each of those scenarios happening, you get a much better idea of the risks and rewards of a proposed course of action.

The Monte Carlo simulation is useful if you want to better understand the implications and ramifications of a particular course of action, strategy, plan or decision. It is especially useful when there is a high degree of uncertainty around some of the assumptions you need to make. For example, if you are considering launching a new product there are many unknown variables to consider. You don't really know how long the product will take to perfect, and you don't know how long it will take to manufacture the product and iron out the glitches. The Monte Carlo simulation could help limit the risk, because you can execute the strategy with more certainty and awareness of the best-case and worst-case scenarios. It is commonly used in fields such as finance, project management, manufacturing, engineering, research and development, insurance, oil and gas and transportation.

Linear programming

Also known as linear optimization, this is a method of identifying the best outcome based on a set of constraints using a linear mathematical model. It allows you to solve problems involving minimizing and maximizing conditions, such as how to maximize profit while minimizing costs. For example, taking the limitations of materials and labour, you could use linear programming to determine the 'best' production levels in order to maximize profits under those conditions.

Clearly, being able to optimize your resources is an important skill in business. Therefore, linear programming is useful if you have a number of constraints, such as time, raw materials, etc, and you wanted to know the best combination or where to direct your resources for maximum profit.

It is essentially a resource allocation process that can help guide decision making and increase revenue. Industries that use this technique effectively include transportation, energy, telecommunications and manufacturing.

Cohort analysis

This is a subset of behavioural analytics, which allows you to study the behaviour of a group over time. The groups or cohorts in this context are aggregations of data points or relevant stakeholders in your business and the data may come from e-commerce platforms, web applications or sales data. The groups being analysed usually share common characteristics so that you can compare cohorts and extract some potentially meaningful insights. The behaviour being assessed can be anything that is of interest to you and your business.

What makes this technique so useful is that it allows you to see patterns in the data more clearly – patterns that would otherwise be missed if the data was not clustered in cohorts. By drilling down into each specific cohort, you can gain a much better understanding of that group's behaviour. Obviously, when you understand what a specific cohort or group is doing, you can modify your approach to improve results.

Cohort analysis is especially useful if you want to know more about the behaviour of a group of stakeholders, such as customers or employees. Rather than having to take a broad-brush look at what all your customers are doing or how they are reacting to a new product or change in service, you can get a much more accurate picture of what's really going on if you divide those stakeholders into groups that share similar features. In this way, cohort analysis can help guide decision making, especially around decisions that could alter behaviour in important stakeholder groups. If, for example, you discover that most of your sales are made to women aged between 35 and 45 then you can tailor your marketing and advertising to further tap into that lucrative market and increase sales.

Factor analysis

This is the collective name given to a group of statistical techniques that are used primarily for data reduction and structure detection. It can reduce the number of variables within data to help make it more useful. In modern business, we are inundated with data, and having too much data can be just as useless and debilitating than having too little. Reducing the variables within the data makes it much easier to detect a structure in the relationships between those variables, which makes the variables easier to classify.

Factor analysis can help you extract insights from huge data sets. It can also help you to identify causal relationships that could direct strategy and improve decision making. Therefore, you should use factor analysis if you need to analyse and understand more about the interrelationships among a large number of variables, and to explain these variables in terms of their common underlying dimensions or factors. If you have gathered a wealth of quantitative and qualitative data about your customers or employees and what they think and feel about your company, this is potentially very useful – but only if you can unravel the interdependencies and appreciate what variables affect what outcome. For example, if you realize that your staff turnover is too high but you are unsure why, you may conduct exit interviews and initiate an employee survey. But that data alone may not tell you very clearly what is happening in the business. By identifying all the salient attributes that you can think of that may be causing the high turnover, you can then use factor analysis to assess the correlations and identify patterns that can help you to solve or at least reduce the problem.

Neural network analysis

A neural network is a computer program modelled on the human brain, which can process a huge amount of information and identify patterns in a similar way that we do. Neural network analysis is therefore the process of analysing the mathematical modelling that makes up a neural network. Because neural networks recognize patterns and learn to improve their recognition ability, their insights can help make predictions. These predications can then be tested and the results used to improve decision making and performance. Neural networks are already used to create models of the human body, allowing healthcare professionals to test out the results of certain medical interventions before they are conducted in the real world. These simulations then provide additional information that can help doctors make the right decisions.

This technique is particularly useful if you have a large amount of data and want to use this to forecast the future. As well as healthcare, neural networks are already widely used in industries such as banking and fraud prevention. In business, neural network analysis can help you improve sales forecasting, customer research, and target marketing. Analysis of neural networks can also be helpful in streamlining manufacturing processes and assessing risk. Note that neural network analysis is a complex analytics methodology that normally requires input from experts in neural network analysis, as well as the use of specialist software.

Meta analytics/literature analysis

Meta analysis is the term that describes the synthesis of previous studies in an area in the hope of identifying patterns, trends or interesting relationships among the pre-existing literature and study results. Essentially, it is the study of previous studies. Conceptually, a meta analysis is a statistical approach that combines data from multiple sources to provide a broader, richer and potentially more accurate insight into the area being studied. Meta analysis becomes more precise and accurate the more data is used.

This technique is useful whenever you want to obtain relevant insights without conducting any studies yourself. So long as the analysis is in the public domain or relatively easy to access, this approach can be considerably cheaper than running your own analysis. Meta analysis could be particularly useful if you were looking to enter a new market or geographic territory. If you don't already operate in that market or territory, then you may be tempted to make assumptions about buying behaviour and the suitability of your products or services to that market. If, however, there have already been some studies conducted on this new market or territory – even if they are focused around different products or services – you could collate these studies and seek to identify patterns of behaviour that could influence your decision making and minimize the risk.

Advanced analytics: machine learning, deep learning and cognitive computing

Above are some of the most commonly used analytic tools that businesses are using today. But more advanced analytics like machine learning, deep learning and cognitive computing are increasingly becoming a part of business decision making and operations. Whether these apply to your business depends on what you're trying to achieve with data – it's fair to say that these are less commonly used than, say, sentiment analysis or business experimentation. However, that is changing. So even if these techniques don't have an application in your business at present, it is worth every business leader being aware of the advanced analytic possibilities.

Machine learning and deep learning involve feeding data into machines, which then decide the best course of action based on that data without human intervention. This means that computers don't have to be explicitly programmed but can change and improve their algorithms by themselves. Thanks to these self-learning algorithms, the machines essentially learn from the data they're given and decide what to do next. Sometimes this decision may prompt some sort of human action (for instance, if something needs repairing or replacing, a human will be tasked with this). Increasingly, though, computers are able to carry out the interventions themselves.

Anyone who remembers taking computer programming classes in school will remember that computers needed an incredibly precise set of instructions to accomplish a task. The more complicated the task, the more complicated the instructions had to be. Machine learning and deep learning are inherently different from traditional programming. Rather than telling a computer exactly how to solve a problem, the programmer instead tells it *how to go about learning to solve the problem* for itself. In a nutshell, it involves applying statistics to learning in order to identify patterns in data and then make predictions from those patterns. The origins of deep learning and machine learning stretch as far back as the 1950s, when computer scientists taught a computer to play checkers. From there, as computational power has increased, so has the complexity of the patterns a computer can recognize and, therefore, the predictions it can make and problems it can solve.

Building upon this, cognitive computing comes from a mashup of cognitive science – the study of the human brain and how it functions – and computer science. The goal of cognitive computing is to simulate human thought processes in a computerized model. So, using self-learning algorithms, the computer can mimic the way the human brain works. While computers have been faster at calculations and processing than humans for decades, they haven't been able to accomplish tasks that humans take for granted as simple, like understanding natural language, or recognizing unique objects in an image. Cognitive computing systems, like IBM's Watson, rely on deep learning algorithms and neural networks to process information by comparing it to a teaching set of data. The more data the system is exposed to, the more it learns, and the more accurate it becomes over time; the neural network is a complex 'tree' of decisions the computer can make to arrive at an answer.

There are five significant ways that advances in machine learning, deep learning and cognitive computing are revolutionizing our world and the way we do business. These are:

1 Machines can see

Because computers are able to look at a large data set and use machine learning algorithms to classify images, it's relatively easy to write an algorithm that can recognize characteristics in a group of images and categorize them appropriately. As discussed in Chapter 2, it takes four highly trained medical pathologists to review a breast cancer scan, decide what they're seeing, and then make a decision about a diagnosis. Now, an algorithm has been written that can detect the cancer more accurately than the best pathologists, freeing the doctors up to make the treatment decisions more quickly and accurately. The same kind of technology is behind driverless cars, because computers can now recognize the difference between a tree and a pedestrian, a red and green traffic light, and a road or a field. This innovation alone could revolutionize many different business models, particularly supply chain and delivery or personal transportation.

2 Machines can read

It's one thing to be able to say whether or not a document contains a certain word or phrase – understanding context is a whole different ball game. Now, algorithms can determine whether a sentence is positive or negative, and more. This type of technology can help us understand more about what people are thinking and feeling, and can save many, many hours of human effort. For example, using Google's street view technology and its ability to read street numbers, the company was able to map all the addresses in France in just a few hours – a feat that would have taken many experienced mapmakers weeks, possibly months, to do manually.

3 Machines can listen...

Siri, Cortana and the like represent a huge leap in machines' understanding of human speech. Now, virtual personal assistants can recognize a huge and ever-growing array of commands and respond in kind. Google and its competitors are even moving towards search algorithms being able to understand natural speech, as voice searching becomes more popular. Today, you can type or speak a natural sentence like, 'Where's the nearest coffee shop that's open right now?' and Google understands not only what you mean, but where you are, what time it is, and how to respond.

4 … and they can talk

Computer language translations are something of a running joke, and for good reason. There are so many nuances to language – slang, idioms, cultural meaning – that simply running a piece of text through translation software can produce some incorrect and very funny results. But new machine learning algorithms are making more accurate, real-time translations possible. Microsoft, for example, now offers real-time translations for Skype video conferencing in seven different languages. In this case, it's the combination of listening to the user speak, understanding the words, and translating them all in real time that's the impressive breakthrough. And because the program is machine learning-based, it will only get better with practice as it has more and more data to work with.

5 Machines can write

As we've seen already in this book, computers are getting a lot better at creative writing – even to the point where they are generating articles for respected news sources. If a computer can recognize something – an image, a document, a file, etc – and describe it accurately, there could be many uses for such automation. This has broad implications for all kinds of data entry and classification tasks that previously required human intervention. While the technology still isn't perfect in many cases, it will get better.

Given the amazing possibilities that already exist and the speed at which these technologies are advancing, I firmly believe machine learning, deep learning and cognitive computing will significantly impact most industries and the jobs within them – which is why every manager should have at least some grasp of these terms. The real promise of deep learning, machine learning and cognitive computing is not that computers will start to think like humans. Rather, it's that, given a large enough data set, fast enough processors, and a sophisticated enough algorithm, computers can begin to accomplish tasks that, before, were only possible for humans. In an analytic sense, this means that increasingly complex data tasks can be performed and optimized autonomously – and this, in turn, leads to deeper insights that translate into better decisions and optimized performance.

Combining analytics for maximum success

Often the value of data is not in any one huge data set or one flashy analytic tool – it's in the insights that can be gained from *combining* different types of data and analytics. For example, correlation analysis may tell you that you sell more Pop-Tarts when there's a hurricane warning, but it won't tell you *why* that is. If you wanted to understand why people turned to Pop-Tarts specifically (say, if you wanted to target similar products), you could carry out some text or sentiment analysis looking at what people say about Pop-Tarts on social media platforms.

The idea behind combining analytics is to base your decision making and business operations on as clear a picture as possible, not just what one set of analysis is telling you. Combining information from more than one source and using different analytic approaches allows you to verify insights from more than one angle.

All the approaches I've outlined in this chapter show only a fraction of the analytic possibilities available to businesses today. Just a few years ago, none of this was possible; we couldn't do sentiment analysis on text, computers couldn't identify cancer better than doctors, and facial recognition software was in its infancy and a long way from being as accurate as the human eye. Analytics in particular has made such huge leaps that no one knows for sure what's going to be possible in ten or even five years' time. Therefore, when developing your data strategy, it's important to stay open to new opportunities that data and analytics may provide further down the road.

Creating the technology and data infrastructure

08

Having decided how you want to use data, what kind of data is best for you, and how you might want to analyse that data, the next step in creating a robust data strategy is considering the technology and infrastructure implications of those decisions. Specifically, this means deciding on the software or hardware that will take data and turn it into insights. Remember, having masses of data at your disposal is meaningless if you don't have the ability to learn something from that data and grow your business as a result. If you're going to get the very most out of data (be it better decision making, improved operational performance, or increased revenue), you will need to invest in some tools or services to make that happen. Most companies have some existing data infrastructure and technology, perhaps in the form of SQL programming, relational databases and data warehouses. These are all well and good, but the developments around big data technology mean that most companies have to rethink their data infrastructure.

Until relatively recently it was difficult for businesses to work with a wide variety and volume of data without making heavy infrastructure investments (expensive software and systems, massive data storage facilities, a team of data analysists, etc). Thankfully, that's no longer the case. Developments like 'big data as a service' (which I discuss below) and the ever-expanding market of data providers have allowed even the smallest company to harness external data sets, resources and skills very easily. Technology advances like cloud computing and distributed storage have also opened up new data possibilities for businesses, allowing them to tap into the power of data without making heavy investments in on-site data storage.

In order to turn data into insights, you'll need to consider the following four infrastructure elements: 1) data collection, 2) data storage, 3) data analysis and processing, and 4) data access and communication. These are generally known as the 'layers' of big data. In this chapter, I look at each layer in turn, exploring the key considerations and commonly used tools.

Given that most companies have some existing data infrastructure in place, as a starting point, it makes sense to consider what technology and systems you already have for each of the four data layers. You will undoubtedly need to make changes and additions to any existing infrastructure, but just keep in mind that some of your existing systems may have a role to play in your data strategy. For example, are you collecting useful data already (perhaps through your website or customer service centre, for instance) but don't yet have the capacity to analyse this fully or communicate insights from that data to the people who need them? Depending on the data you intend to use, could your existing data storage facilities be improved or supplemented to cope with that data? Can your existing analytics capabilities play a role? Are you already communicating information across the company successfully, and, if so, how? These are all things to consider.

Also, keep in mind that you may not need to invest in infrastructure elements for each of the four layers. If you are purchasing access to external data (like Facebook) to improve your marketing decisions, then the data capture, storage and analysis elements may not apply to you – or they may apply to a lesser extent (if, say, you want to combine this external data with your own internal data). Your infrastructure requirements will depend very much on how you are looking to use data, what data you want to work with, and how you need to interrogate that data. As such, each company's setup is unique and there is no one-size-fits-all approach. Simply work through each of the layers in order, note your existing capabilities and build a list of your requirements as you go.

'Big data as a service': the one-stop solution for businesses?

In the last few years, many new businesses have emerged offering cloud-based data services to business customers. This fast-growing new market is commonly known as 'big data as a service' (BDaaS). In practice, the term BDaaS can refer to a wide variety of data functions, from supplying data to supplying analytical tools to carrying out the actual analysis for the customer and providing insights via reports. Some BDaaS providers extend to data consulting and advisory services.

It's becoming a lucrative market. Some estimate that the portion of business IT spending that is cloud-based, x-as-a-service-type activity will increase from about 15 per cent today to 35 per cent by 2021. Considering the global big data market is estimated to grow to US $88 billion by 2021, the BDaaS market could account for around $30 billion of that.

There are some significant advantages to BDaaS, not least the fact that even very small businesses can benefit from absolutely vast data sets that they may otherwise not be able to access. BDaaS also drastically lowers or eliminates upfront infrastructure costs, thereby lowering the barrier of entry and removing many of the hurdles associated with implementing a data strategy. With BDaaS, you simply rent the provider's cloud-based storage and analytics services and pay as you go. In addition, when you work with a BDaaS provider, in theory, all of the technical issues and requirements are 'behind the scenes' and handled by the provider – leaving you free to concentrate on the insights gleaned from the data. Another great advantage is that BDaaS providers often take on the cost of data governance, compliance and protection – which may be particularly attractive to smaller businesses.

Many of the big corporations like HP and IBM are now offering their own versions of BDaaS. HP's analytics platform, Haven, is now available entirely through the cloud, meaning that storage, analytics and reporting are all handled by HP systems and you simply purchase a subscription to use the platform, thereby eliminating other infrastructure costs. Likewise, IBM's Analytics for Twitter service provides businesses with access to data and analytics on Twitter's 500 million tweets per day and more than 300 million monthly active users. IBM provides its own analytical tools and applications for making sense of all that unstructured data, and has trained an army of consultants to help businesses profit from it.

Agricultural manufacturer John Deere is another example of a big corporation providing its own version of BDaaS. As we know, sensors fitted into John Deere tractors gather data about the machinery as well as soil and crop conditions. This data is streamed to the company's MyJohnDeere.com and Farmsight platforms. Farmers can subscribe to access analytical intelligence on everything from when to order spare parts to where to plant crops, saving them the burden of setting up their own analytic infrastructure.

BDaaS is increasingly playing its part in sales and marketing, too. As we saw in Chapter 5, Acxiom is the world's biggest seller of direct marketing data. By applying analytics to the massive amount of personal data they collect, they can more effectively profile consumers and hand their own customers potential leads. Amazon Web Services and Google's AdSense and AdWords are better-known services that also fall under the banner of BDaaS.

BDaaS is a fantastic option if you're looking to understand more about your customers, markets and trends, and make better decisions based on this information. However, it's not ideal if you want to use data to improve your operations or if you intend to monetize data. In these cases, it is almost always better to invest in the technology to capture your own data, which, in turn, means you'll need the technology to store and analyse that data. Essentially, whenever data is going to be a vital part of your everyday operations and processes, you are better off maintaining ownership and control of that data, rather than relying on external providers. However, this doesn't mean you need to spend a fortune – as we'll see later in the chapter, there are many low-cost options like open source software that can help keep infrastructure costs down.

Though it may not be suited to every business, the concept of BDaaS is rock solid – and it's something that will become more popular and prevalent. As more and more companies realize the worth of implementing data strategies, it makes sense that more services will emerge to support them.

Collecting data

The data source or data collection layer is where the data arrives at your company, whether it is internal or external data, structured or unstructured. This includes data from your sales records, customer database, customer and employee feedback, social media channels, marketing lists, e-mail archives and any data gleaned from monitoring or measuring aspects of your operations. You may already have the data you need to achieve your strategic objectives, but it is more likely that you will need to source some or all of the data required – and sourcing new data may lead to new infrastructure investments. Today there are more sophisticated tools for capturing data than ever before, particularly thanks to the IoT. Sensors, for example, being very small and relatively inexpensive, can be built into pretty much anything, and this has revolutionized data projects for many businesses. In the past, for example, if a haulage company wanted to track data from delivery trucks, they would have to invest in costly telematics systems. Now, the same functionality can be delivered with smartphone apps. The average smartphone now includes highly sensitive and accurate sensors as standard, giving a wealth of data, such as GPS location data, speed of travel, etc.

Exactly what tools or systems you need for capturing data will depend on the types of data you have selected, but key options include the following: sensors (these could be fitted to devices, machines, buildings, vehicles, packaging, or anywhere else you would like to capture data from – even employee name tags, frying pans and yoga mats!); apps which generate user data (for example, an app which allows customers to browse and order more easily); CCTV video; beacons (such as iBeacons from Apple, which allows you to capture and transmit data to and from mobile phones – especially useful if you want to monitor footfall); website cookies tracking how people use your site; changes to your website that prompt customers for more information; and social media profiles. As for capturing the data, you can either set up the data capture systems yourself in-house or you can hire a data company to capture the data on your behalf.

Of course, if you choose to access external data sources (be it freely available data like census data or premium, paid-for data like customer segment data), you may not have to make any infrastructure changes at all, since you're accessing someone else's data. Again, it depends on how you are wanting to use the data. If you're seeking operational improvements or to monetize data, it makes sense to have your own systems in place.

Here's an innovative example of capturing data from an unlikely source: a golf swing. A recent study commissioned by GolfTEC set out to identify, through big data, what it is that differentiates pro golfers from average golfers.[1] Using state-of-the-art motion sensors, cameras and monitors, the SwingTRU study captured 225 terabytes of data from over 13,000 golf swings from golfers of all abilities: from PGA pros to handicap 30 golfers. So much of golf instruction comes down to gut instinct or opinion rather than outright fact. This means a coach is likely to make judgements and decisions based on their own experiences and understanding rather than on solid statistics – generally because the data is not always available. So, taking 10 different golf lessons from 10 different instructors could easily lead to receiving 10 different ideas about how to best improve your drive. But, by measuring each golfer's swing, players can get an accurate, fact-based analysis of their game.

Interestingly, the study found that there are six key differences between exceptional and mediocre golfers, such as hip sway at the top of the swing, shoulder tilt at the point of impact, and hip turn at the point of impact. Specifically, the study claimed to identify the *precise* difference in each of these metrics between players at either end of the ability scale. So, by comparing how his or her own statistics compare with those of each of the reference players, anyone can see where they sit on the scale, as well as what they should be aiming to improve.

Although GolfTEC sampled 13,000 swings for this study, the company says it has collected data from an impressive 90 million swings during its

20-year history. The technology has certainly evolved during this time – the earliest data collection was done using a system involving gyroscopes and metal bars attached to players, which were time consuming to fit (not to mention somewhat invasive for the poor golfers). The current method puts the player who is being measured within a magnetic field, where movements can be measured to within a hundredth of a degree of accuracy. GolfTEC say that the study is just 'version one' and there are many plans to increase the scope of their data collection in future. And this is a good lesson for any company to keep in mind – as the technology for capturing data evolves, so too should a company's data strategy.

Let's revisit a couple of examples from earlier in the book to see how other companies are collecting data. As we saw in Chapter 4, ShotSpotter has integrated microphones into GE's Intelligent LED Smart City street lights in order to capture the sounds of gunfire in urban zones. Interestingly, much of the technology to pinpoint gunfire already existed in GE's lights, including GPS, and analogue-to-digital converters. All ShotSpotter needed to add was the actual microphones to capture sounds. This is a great example of enhancing existing capabilities and systems, instead of reinventing the wheel.

Transport for London (also in Chapter 4) shows us how capturing data from a variety of sources creates a rich picture of insights. TfL collect data through their ticketing systems, sensors attached to vehicles and traffic signals, customer surveys and focus groups and, of course, social media. As Lauren Sager Weinstein told me, 'We use information from the back-office systems for processing contactless payments, as well as Oyster, train location and traffic signal data, cycle hire and the congestion charge.'

Storing data

Having identified your data capture needs, you need to think about where you will keep your data. The main storage options include traditional in-house solutions like a company server or computer hard disk, distributed or cloud-based storage systems, data warehouses, and data lakes.

Regular hard disks are available at very high capacities and for very little cost these days and, likewise, in-house servers can be a cost-effective solution. If you're a small business or you're not looking to store a large amount of complex data, then a traditional solution like this may be all you need. But if you do need to store (and analyse) a large amount of data, or if data is going to be an essential part of your business operations, you will almost certainly need a more sophisticated setup. Luckily, as the volume and variety of data generated and stored by companies have expanded, so too has the range of sophisticated but accessible systems and tools designed to help companies with this task.

Sophisticated doesn't have to mean huge financial investment. Free open-source software exists for most of the essential big data tasks, including storage. And distributed storage systems are designed to run on cheap, off-the-shelf hardware which is readily available. Today, any company can use off-the-shelf hardware and open-source software to store and analyse data, providing they spend time developing the skills and knowledge to setup and run these systems. Unfortunately, that's the trade-off with free open-source software: it takes time and a certain degree of technical skill to get it all set up and working the way you need. If you don't have the expertise in-house or your strategic timetable doesn't allow you to invest the time in developing these tools, then a paid-for solution that can get down to business straight away will be more suitable. 'Enterprise' versions are available for many of the open-source tools; these are usually customized versions of the free packages, designed to be easier to set up and use, or specifically targeted at various industries.

Understanding cloud-based/distributed storage systems

Distributed/cloud storage is increasingly becoming the go-to solution for many businesses, because it is incredibly flexible (it's easy to create additional storage when needed), and you don't need to have physical data storage systems on site. It is also considerably cheaper and more accessible than investing in expensive dedicated systems and data warehouses.

In simplistic terms, 'distributed storage' means using cheap, off-the-shelf components to create high-capacity data storage, which is controlled by software that keeps track of where everything is, and finds it for you when you need it. 'Cloud storage' simply means that your data is stored (usually) remotely, but connected to the Internet, so that it is accessible from anywhere with an Internet connection. Most distributed storage systems make use of cloud technology and the terms 'distributed storage' and 'cloud storage' are often used interchangeably.

Before the cloud, computers could still be linked together on a company network, but the storage capacity and computing power was limited to the company's own in-house hardware (and physical space and budget). When a business wanted to increase their storage, they had to get rid of old files or buy new hardware. Cloud computing, on the other hand, enables any business to increase their storage capacity without having to buy new hardware. The cloud is all about using the power of lots of different computers to perform tasks. This means that large volumes of data can be stored using many different computers, often in completely different locations, which are all connected via the Internet. This and the increasing connectivity of devices (the IoT) has paved the way for the data explosion we've seen in recent years.

Using cloud technology, a distributed storage system allows data to be stored on many different computers, so that individual computers perform only small parts of the overall computing task. This spreads the load and makes storing huge amounts of data cheaper, easier and much more efficient. Using distributed systems, you can store data anywhere and still find and access it quickly and easily. This has transformed the amount as well as the variety of data that businesses can work with. With dramatically increased storage capabilities, we can store and analyse data, such as video data, that was previously too big to store in large quantities. And, because the underlying principle of distributed storage is to spread the computing load across many different computers, this in itself makes analysing data easier.

What about data security, though? Many people assume that the cloud is less secure than storing data on a private company server. I'd argue that, in many cases, cloud storage is actually more secure than keeping it all in-house. With an in-house server, the data is stored in one place and one place only (bringing to mind the phrase 'keeping all your eggs in one basket'). If you're relying on data for key business operations, this may be risky. Any form of business disruption (fire, theft, extreme weather, to name just a few) could result in temporary loss of access to the data or, worst case scenario, complete loss of the data. With cloud storage, however, the data is replicated in more than one place and can be accessed anywhere via the Internet.

Introducing Hadoop

Today, Hadoop is the most widely used system for providing data storage and processing across 'commodity' hardware – meaning off-the-shelf components being linked together, as opposed to expensive, bespoke systems custom made for an organization. Released in 2005 by the Apache Software Foundation, Hadoop is a set of open-source programs and procedures which anyone can use as the 'backbone' of their data infrastructure. As you would expect of any distributed system, it is highly flexible, allowing businesses to expand and adjust their data storage and analysis as needed.

It's estimated that more than half of Fortune 500 companies use Hadoop, including pretty much all the big online names. And, it being an open-source solution, anyone is free to alter it for their own purposes; modifications made to the software by expert engineers at, for example, Google, are fed back to the development community, where they are often used to improve the 'official' product. This form of collaborative development between volunteer and commercial users is a key feature of open-source software.

Hadoop is made up of 'modules', with the two most important modules being its distributed file system and MapReduce. The distributed file system allows data to be stored in an easily accessible format. Hadoop uses its own file system which sits 'above' the host computer's own file system, meaning the system can be accessed using almost any computer, so long as it runs a supporting operating system. MapReduce provides the basic tools for processing and analysing data. It's named after the two basic operations this module carries out: the 'map' meaning locating data and putting it into a format suitable for analysis, and the 'reduce' meaning to perform a mathematical operation (such as counting the number of men aged 30–45 in a customer database).

A distributed system like Hadoop allows you to store massive amounts of data. Walmart, for example, has a real-time transactional database consisting of 40 petabytes of data – and that's just transactional data from the *most recent weeks*. Data from all across the chain's stores, online divisions and corporate units is all stored on a Hadoop distributed data storage and management system. Facebook, too, has a distributed storage system based on Hadoop's HBase platform to store its mountains of data.

In its raw state, using the basic open-source modules supplied by Apache, Hadoop can be very complex, even for IT professionals. For this reason, many commercial versions (such as Cloudera and Amazon Web Services) have been developed which simplify the task of installing and running a Hadoop system, as well as offering training for in-house staff and ongoing support services. Unless you have a great deal of technical skill in-house, one of the commercial versions may be the most sensible route for you; there's more on this further on in this chapter.

Spark: an alternative to Hadoop

Like Hadoop, Spark is a framework that provides a number of connected platforms and systems for storing and working with data. Also, like Hadoop, Spark is an open source system developed by the Apache Software Foundation.

Many industry insiders see Spark as a more advanced product than Hadoop, largely because it is designed to process data in chunks 'in memory'. This means it transfers data from the physical, magnetic hard disks into much faster electronic memory where processing can be carried out far more quickly – up to 100 times faster in some operations. In fact, in 2014, Spark set a world record by completing a benchmark test involving sorting 100 terabytes of data in 23 minutes – beating the previous world record of 71 minutes held by Hadoop. Its speed has made Spark a popular choice with companies requiring multi-petabyte data storage and analysis. It also makes it highly suited to machine learning applications. Another crucial element of the framework is Spark Streaming, which provides the foundation for performing analytics on streaming, real-time data – such as automatically analysing CCTV footage or social media data on the fly. This makes Spark a very attractive option for any organization seeking to analyse data in real time. For example, in marketing, ads can be targeted based on a user's behaviour at that precise moment, rather than on historical behaviour.

As with Hadoop, in order to make the technology more accessible to businesses, many vendors provide their own commercial versions of Spark. These may be geared towards particular industries, or custom-configured for individual clients, and may include consultancy and support services.

A quick word on data lakes vs data warehouses

In a traditional data warehouse, everything is archived and ordered in a defined way – the products are inside containers, the containers on shelves, the shelves are in rows, and so on. This is the way data warehouses have been organized for years, and it has proved a successful method. In a data warehouse, the data is organized in a hierarchical, logical way that is structured and fixed.

However, there has been a lot of talk in the last couple of years about an alternative to the traditional data warehouse: the data lake. In a data lake, the data is just poured in, in an unstructured way, in its rawest form – fresh from capture, and unadulterated by processing or analysis. This makes data lakes more agile than warehouses, because the data can be configured or reconfigured as necessary, depending on the job you want to do with it. In a data lake, each individual piece of data is treated as an object in its own right and no piece of data is 'higher-level' than any other. Instead of being a hierarchically archived system, like a warehouse, it's basically a big free-for-all. There are some obvious advantages to the data lake approach.

Data stored without any predetermined structure can be more quickly shaped into whatever form is needed. It can then be interrogated via whatever tool is best for the job. However, there are big security implications to consider if you're going to keep all your company data in one place.

Right now, it's still early days and few large corporations have made the leap to keeping all of their data in a lake. But data lakes are expected to become more popular as more businesses seek greater agility and flexibility with their data. For this reason alone, it's worth keeping the data lake in mind as a potential future option.

Analysing and processing data

Having decided on your data collection and storage needs, you now need to consider how you will process and analyse your data to extract information. Therefore, this layer is all about the tools needed to turn data into insights. Specifically, this comes down to programming languages and analytic software.

As with data storage, there's a lot of open-source technology available for processing and analysing data. By tapping into open-source options, you can remove the need for heavy investment in expensive bespoke data analysis infrastructure. But open source is not just for those on a budget. There is a broad trend towards even the biggest corporations adopting open-source technology. With open source, you aren't locked into a particular package or provider, which is an important consideration if data is a critical business asset. When your data flows through an open-source system, you can easily change vendors or providers without a great deal of upheaval.

The process of extracting insights from data boils down to three steps: 1) preparing the data (identifying, cleaning and formatting the data so you can analyse it more easily); 2) building the analytic model; and 3) drawing a conclusion from the insights gained. A common method for analysing data is using a MapReduce tool, which I mentioned earlier in the chapter. Essentially, this is used to select the elements of the data that you want to analyse and put it into a format from which insights can be gleaned. Commercial software exists from big vendors such as IBM, Oracle and Google to help you turn data into insights. Google has BigQuery, which is designed to let anyone with a bit of data science knowledge run queries against vast data sets. There are also options like Cloudera, Microsoft HDInsight and Amazon Web Services. In addition, many startups are piling into the market, offering simple solutions which claim to let you simply feed them with all of your data, and sit back while they highlight the most important insights and suggest actions for you to take. Most commercial offerings use the Hadoop framework as the basis and build on it for analysis.

Below I explore some of the best and most widely used analytic services on the market today. As with any commercial product in a competitive market, each has its advantages and disadvantages, so you'll need to consider carefully which best suits your needs. Having said that, all are highly regarded and popular choices!

Amazon Web Services

Amazon packages up the behind-the-scenes magic that makes their business run so smoothly and sells this to other companies. The Amazon business model was based on big data from the start – using personal information to offer a personalized shopping experience. Amazon Web Services includes its Elastic Cloud Compute and Elastic MapReduce services to offer large-scale data storage and analysis in the cloud.

Cloudera CDH

Cloudera was formed by former employees of Google, Yahoo, Facebook and Oracle and offers open-source as well as commercial Hadoop-based big data solutions. Their distributions make use of their Impala analytics engine, which has also been adopted and included in packages offered by competitors such as Amazon and MapR.

Hortonworks Data Platform

Unlike every other big analytics platform, HDP comprises entirely open-source code, with all of its elements built through the Apache Software Foundation. They make their money offering services and support getting it running and providing the results you're after.

Infobright

This database management system is available as both an open-source, free edition and a paid-for proprietary version. The product is geared specifically towards users working with the IoT. They offer three levels of service for paid users, with higher-tier customers given access to the helpdesk and quicker e-mail support response times.

IBM Big Data Platform

IBM offers a range of products and services designed to make complex big data analysis more accessible to businesses. They offer their own Hadoop distribution known as InfoSphere BigInsights.

IBM Watson

Watson, which first gained fame by winning the US TV gameshow Jeopardy! in 2011, is IBM's cognitive computing and machine learning offering, using natural language processing technology. Watson works in a probabilistic manner: ask it a question and it will return a series of likely answers, ranked according to their likelihood of being correct. Over 300 partner organizations are already working with IBM and Watson across industries as diverse as healthcare, marketing, retail and finance. In Chapter 3 we saw how IBM's Watson was helping Wimbledon tournament organizers better position their content in line with what fans want to read. By crunching through hundreds of thousands of social media and online posts which are related to the tournament, Watson was able to identify the stories that fans are most engaged with and help the content team create exactly the sort of content fans wanted to see.

MapR

MapR offer their own distribution of Hadoop, notably different from others as it replaces the commonly used Hadoop File System with its alternative MapR Data Platform, which it claims offers better performance and ease of use.

Microsoft HDInsight

Microsoft's flagship analytical offering, HDInsight, is based on Hortonworks Data Platform, but tailored to work with their own Azure cloud services and SQL Server database management system. A big advantage for businesses is that it integrates with Excel, meaning even staff with only basic IT skills can have a go at big data analytics.

Pivotal Big Data Suite

Pivotal's big data package comprises their own Hadoop distribution, Pivotal HD, and their analytics platform, Pivotal Analytics. The business model allows consumers to store an unlimited amount of data and pay a subscription fee which varies according to how much they analyse. The company is strongly invested in the data lake philosophy of a unified, object-based storage repository for all of an organization's data.

Splunk Enterprise

This platform is specifically geared to businesses that generate a lot of their own data through their own machinery. Their stated goal is 'machine data to operational intelligence' and the IoT is key to their strategy. Their analytics drives Domino's Pizza's US coupon campaigns.

The beauty of big data right now is the ever-increasing range of analytic options that are opening up for businesses. Even if you're starting from scratch with data, or have little in-house technical expertise, or a very limited budget, or work in a highly specialized field, the right analytic option is within reach.

Providing access to data

The final layer of any data infrastructure is about providing access to data to the people (or even machines) that need it, and the tools and systems that make this possible. Ultimately, it's about putting systems or processes in place for making sure insights are easily accessible (and understandable) so that they can lead to business improvements. Visualizing and communicating data is one aspect of this, but so is deciding who should be allowed access to what data, controlling that access, and ensuring good data stewardship.

As we saw in Chapter 3, there is a trend towards widespread data access in many organizations, meaning people right across the company can access data and use that as the basis of their decisions. As such, there's a lot of emphasis on self-service BI reporting, giving people the ability to choose how they want to interrogate data and get to the insights they need by themselves, as opposed to simply dishing up standard BI reports. Companies like Citibank and Walmart are creating corporate data hubs to give their people access to billions of data points. At online retailer Etsy, an impressive 80 per cent of the workforce now access and use the company's huge amount of transactional and browsing data to make better decisions and provide a more personalized shopping experience for customers. Depending on the specifics of your business, you may also need to allow access to data for external users and customers, and this needs careful consideration. For example, Etsy shares its clickstream data with Etsy sellers through its Shop

Stats system, allowing sellers to carry out their own analysis and hopefully increase their own revenues (and, in turn, Etsy's share of the sale). Likewise, John Deere's MyJohnDeere.com online portal allows farmers to access data gathered from sensors attached to their machines, as well as aggregated data from other farmers around the world. And IBM's work with Wimbledon organizers shows how data can be accessed by a range of users, from internal marketing teams and in-house staff creating content to journalists and external fans. The IBM Slamtracker statistics interface, which used to run as a standalone app within the tournament website, has now been integrated across the tournament's media output. Insights from the system can now be used across all channels, including being shared across social media platforms and embedded in match reports. This increased access makes the data more useful and meaningful for a wider range of users.

Considering data stewardship

Data has gone way beyond the realms of being 'just an IT thing'. Today's smart companies implement company-wide data strategies and aim to engage all staff with data-driven decision making and operations. But when increasing numbers of staff are engaged with data, and large numbers are actually interacting with the company's data on a regular basis, who is responsible for managing the data? In these circumstances, the traditional model of a data team being the only people responsible for looking after data is starting to seem outdated. Data stewardship, or giving all staff who work with data the responsibility of managing it properly, provides the answer.

When genealogy website Ancestry.com restructured its data operations, the primary goal was to move from daily batch processing of data to real-time, on-the-fly processing. However, an unexpected by-product was an increased understanding of how data was used throughout the business. When data isn't properly looked after, it becomes meaningless and valueless. Even worse, if the data is out of date, incorrectly categorized, or used out of context, it can lead to misinformed decisions that can damage the long-term health of the company. Missing and mismatched metadata can cause serious problems for a business such as Ancestry, with a database containing over 13 billion records spread across more than 10 petabytes of storage. As Chris Sanders, Director of Data Warehouse and Visualization at Ancestry.com, explained, 'We ran into problems where data just didn't exist or it was inaccurate. For data warehousing, business intelligence, reporting and legal obligations, or to pay royalties, that's a nightmare.' Now, all Ancestry.com staff who work with data are encouraged to be data stewards, responsible for maintaining the accuracy of data as they interact with it.

I can certainly see Ancestry's approach becoming more and more popular as businesses find themselves dealing with an ever-increasing amount of data, touching on the workload of a greater number of employees. Data stewardship – when it is rolled out throughout a business – reduces the risks posed by bad, out-of-date or inaccurate information. For that reason, I can see it become a popular approach for businesses striving to maintain a competitive edge.

Communicating data

There are various methods for communicating data to the people or machines that need them. Ultimately, you need a method of communication (however fancy or simple) that highlights insights and shows how decisions and actions based on the data can lead to business improvements.

If you're using data to make better business decisions, simple graphics and reports are an effective way to get insights to the people who need them, and should require no additional infrastructure investment. In a small business, this may be all you need. There are some tips to help with communicating data in simple reports/charts in Chapter 3 but, essentially, the communication just needs to be clear and concise. This means don't bury precious nuggets of information in a 50-page report or a complicated chart that no one understands. If the key insights aren't clearly presented, they won't result in action.

For more complex communication needs, commercial data visualization platforms make data attractive and easy to understand. The rise of data and analytics has brought with it a wave of new visualization tools capable of making the outputs of the analytics look pretty, and improving understanding and speed of comprehension. Many of the analytics platforms mentioned earlier in the chapter have some sort of visualization function included, so there's no need to invest in additional systems. However, if they don't meet your needs, there are some excellent cloud-based visualization tools which are relatively easy to use, such as QlikView and Tableau (which are paid-for tools).

Self-service BI reporting and management dashboards are a great option whenever you want your people to be able to interrogate the data and extract their own insights. Whether you decide to report results through traditional reporting that utilizes some data visualization techniques or whether you opt for management dashboards and/or infographics will very often depend on your in-house expertise. Keep in mind, however, that any good reporting or dashboard system, no matter how complex or fancy it is, should still make it easy to understand the key *insights* needed to improve business performance. Many of the same rules that apply to communicating and visualizing data in simple reports and graphics apply here, such as including headlines and a mixture of narrative and visuals.

At the more complex end of the scale, automated machine-to-machine (M2M) communication is an increasingly important aspect of data communication, and should be considered in any data strategy. Indeed, it's a vital component of any IoT-related products or services since M2M communication is what allows devices to exchange data. M2M communication tools and systems can range from algorithms that tell your website to recommend product X if a customer buys product Y, to stock management systems that automatically order more stock when a certain level is reached, to security systems issuing an alert when certain behaviour is detected. As the technology develops rapidly, the range of options and applications in this field is growing at an unprecedented rate.

Building a big data infrastructure is a complex undertaking, and there are many variables to consider. I hope this chapter has given you a good understanding of the key infrastructure elements. As with any aspect of data, if you're still unsure where to start, or which option might be best for your needs, then I recommend working with a big data consultant or taking advantage of the consultancy services that come with many of the commercial big data packages.

Endnote

1 Bernard Marr (2016) How big data unlocked the 6 secrets of the perfect golf swing, *Forbes*, 15 July, available at: http://www.forbes.com/sites/bernardmarr/ 2016/07/15/how-big-data-unlocked-the-6-secrets-of-the-perfect-golf-swing/ #156d26f3539b

Building data competencies in your organization

09

So far, we have talked about the data itself and the tools, technology and infrastructure requirements for making sense of data. However, there's another vital ingredient that every business must consider as part of their data strategy: developing the right data skills and competencies. In order to get the most out of data it is essential to cultivate certain skills. Of course, data analysis skills are crucial, but so is the ability to relate data to the business's needs, or communicate key insights from data to people with no technical background.

There are two main routes to developing data-related competencies. One is boosting your in-house talent (either through hiring data scientists or investing in training your existing people), and the other is outsourcing the data analysis (either by partnering with an external data provider or by crowdsourcing your analytics needs). Both routes are explored in this chapter.

From a data strategy point of view, there is no one-size-fits-all approach to building data competencies in your organization. You will need to be guided by your strategic goals and limitations such as time and budget. You may, for example, seek to train some of your people in analytics, but also need to partner with an external partner while your own people build their knowledge. You may build and nurture data skills in-house which perfectly suit your everyday decision making and operations, but you may then need some external analytics manpower for a one-off data project further down the line. I recommend you start by looking at the key data competencies outlined in this chapter, identify the gaps in your organization and then build your wish list of how you would ideally fill those gaps.

The big data skill shortage, and what it means for your business

Data skills are in short supply, especially when it comes to big data and emerging technologies and applications such as machine learning, AI and predictive analytics. Demand for big data expertise is growing every day, as more and more companies want to exploit the power of data. Unfortunately, though, the number of people trained to work with data (especially large quantities of data or particularly complex data) and turn that data into insights simply isn't growing in line with the demand. This creates a challenge for companies looking to tap into data skills; with data skills in high demand it can be difficult to attract good people, especially for smaller and mid-sized companies who struggle to compete with the big corporations on wages and benefits. In fact, a 2016 survey found that more than half of business leaders queried felt their ability to carry out analytics was hampered by difficulties in finding the right talent.[1] Overcoming this problem is a challenge that all companies will have to face, hence the rise of more creative solutions like crowdsourcing data analysis (more on this later in the chapter).

To compound the problem of hiring good talent, the role of 'data scientist' is poorly defined, and can be used to describe anyone from a data engineer who sets up the behind-the-scenes systems that collect and store data to statisticians who crunch numbers. For example, I've seen business analysts with no understanding of big data technology or programming languages call themselves data scientists. And I've also seen plenty of programmers call themselves data scientists, even though they lack the business skills that are necessary to turn data into insights. I believe a true data scientist should not only understand the data and computer science aspects, but also possess critical business and analytical skills. The ultimate combination of skills can be hard to find, and it may make more sense to combine skills in a more creative way that works for your business – again, more on that later in the chapter.

There are signs that the skills gap will close. As the buzz around big data and analytics attracts greater attention, more people are being drawn to a career in data science. The *Harvard Business Review* has even gone so far as to name 'data scientist' as the sexiest job of the 21st century[2] (evangelical about data as I am, I still raised an eyebrow at this). And according to users of Glassdoor.com, which allows employees to anonymously rate their jobs and their employers, data scientist is the best job in America. The job came out with the overall best score in Glassdoor's 2016 report, and this will hopefully help attract much-needed fresh talent to the industry.[3]

To some, it might seem surprising to pick data scientist as the best job in America. Sure, it is well paid and high demand for skills means the best candidates have their pick of the top jobs and employers – but it doesn't exactly have a glamorous reputation. Most people picture the role of a data scientist as being stuck at a desk crunching numbers all day. However, in reality, the day-to-day life of a data scientist can be incredibly varied and interesting, as several well-established data experts are keen to point out. Gregg Gordon, vice president of the big data practice group at Kronos, says, 'It's not sitting in a room all day – we take our work and apply it to customer problems. We're working and interacting with customers on a daily basis talking about real problems, then attempting to replicate, model and solve them.' Alex Krowitz, one of Gordon's team members and a 20-year veteran of data science, certainly agrees: 'It's rewarding because you get to see the customer's eyes when they realize you can provide a comprehensive analysis of their whole business.'

The appeal of solving real-life problems with practical solutions is clearly an attractive part of the modern data scientist's work. Particularly when working with very fast, very large incoming data sets to solve problems in real time, as they occur, results are often instantaneously visible, and this can be incredibly rewarding. But even when results occur over a longer period of time, the impact that data can have on a business, and the scope for positive change, is becoming a big draw. Mark Schwarz, VP of data science at Square Root, told me:

> Back in 2003 I wanted to work in data science so I could stand in an elevator next to a sales or operations VP and be able to succinctly explain to them what I did every day. I was a technical expert but virtually all of my time was spent collecting data. We all assumed that someone, somewhere was going to then make good use of that data to drive the business forward in thoughtful ways. In most cases, actually no one was. I moved to more and more data-focused roles to actually put that data collection to use. I wanted to be able to stand next to a VP and say, 'Here's how my team grew revenue or profits.' Now I get to do that.

So the hope is that more and more people will be attracted to a career in data science. Education providers are certainly starting to catch on to this notion, laying the groundwork for a wealth of highly qualified, knowledgeable data scientists for businesses to choose from. In 10 years' time, we may be looking at a very different dynamic, where demand for data scientists no longer outstrips supply. For now, though, the skills shortage is something that every business will need to factor into their considerations.

Building internal skills and competencies

As you will have gathered by now, getting the most out of data is about more than programming or analytics skills. The best technical wizardry in the world means very little without a solid understanding of the wider business context and what the organization is trying to achieve. With this in mind, I set out below the skills that I believe are essential for any organization to nurture, whether that means recruiting new talent to fill skills gaps, or building these skills in your existing talent. The trick is to build teams with the right blend of skills that works for your organization. That may, for example, mean partnering someone with the relevant analytics skills with someone who is great at communicating insights to a wide audience.

Five essential data science skills

One of the questions I get asked the most is, 'What are the most important data skills?' Based on my experience, I believe the following five skills are the most critical for turning data into insights:

1 Business skills
   Any data scientist worth their salt should have a thorough understanding of what keeps the business ticking, what causes it to grow, and whether it's heading in the right direction. This includes an understanding of key business processes, objectives, and core metrics that are used to evaluate the company's performance, as well as what makes the company stand out against its competitors (and, if it doesn't stand out, why not and what needs to change?). Communication skills are also a vital component of extracting the maximum amount of value from data, from strong interpersonal skills to the ability to present findings from data in a clear, compelling way.

2 Analytical skills
   The ability to spot patterns, discern the link between cause and effect, and build simulated models which can be warped and woven until they produce the desired results are all important skills. This includes a solid grounding in industry-standard analytics packages such as SAS Analytics, IBM Predictive Analytics and Oracle Data Mining, as well as a thorough understanding of interpreting reports and visualizations to spot the answers to key business questions.

3 Computer science

Computers are the backbone of any data strategy, so this broad category covers everything from plugging together the cables to creating sophisticated machine learning and natural language processing algorithms. In particular, candidates with a firm grasp of key open source technologies like Hadoop are in demand, as these are the foundations of many organizations' data plans.

4 Statistics and mathematics

A statistician's skills inform just about every aspect of an organization's data operations, from defining relevant populations and appropriate sample sizes at the start of a simulation to reporting the results at the end. A basic grasp of statistics is therefore essential, but a more thorough education in the subject is highly desirable. Mathematics, too, is always useful because, despite the huge increase in the amount of unstructured and semi-structured data we are analysing, most of it still comes out as good old-fashioned numbers.

5 Creativity

This is vital when working with big data. After all, it's an emerging science and there are no hard and fast rules about what a company should use big data for. In this sense, creativity is the ability to apply the technical skillsets mentioned above and use them to produce something of worth (such as an insight) in a way other than following a pre-determined formula. Anyone can be formulaic – today, businesses want innovation that will set them apart from the pack, both in terms of their corporate results and the image they present to their consumers. With the explosion in the number of organizations leveraging data for insights, the ability to come up with new, creative ways of working with data is a very desirable skill indeed.

This diversification of skillsets is something we're seeing across the whole big data industry. As Tye Rattenbury, director of data science at Trifacta, told me:

> If you look at a data science job description from five years ago, it was basically 'advanced degree, computer skills, predictive modelling'. Now that's only a third of it – the other two-thirds are 'works well with others', 'knows how to report and communicate'...

As organizations seek to get more and more from data, it is only natural that we expect more from the people working with data. Rattenbury agrees:

'It's great when people are smart and can do clever stuff, but they need to be able to feed it back into the business so we can do something about it.'

The increasing diversification of skillsets is also partly a result of the way organizations are structured these days. Whereas data science would have previously been an isolated pool of talent, located firmly within the realm of IT, now it is starting to permeate individual departments across organizations. As Rattenbury explains, 'The modern version is about taking that centralized data science team and flat-out splintering them – saying two of these data scientists are going to marketing, one to product design, one to sales... and they're going to be fully embedded in those teams.'

Recruiting new talent

If data is going to be a core part of your business and you have a decent recruitment budget, then hiring data scientists is a worthwhile investment. If you can find candidates with all five traits listed above, then they are likely to deliver great value to your company. In my experience, though, going out and recruiting data scientists with all these skills is the most expensive and difficult option for many companies. You will be up against stiff competition, and you still may not end up with the competencies and teams you really need. Therefore, while all five skills are vital for extracting maximum value from data, you may need to get a little creative with your recruiting.

It may, for example, make more sense to recruit people that have strong analytical skills – like mathematicians, people with quantitative degrees or those with a background in statistics – and then train them in the big data tools you are using. Or you may have a candidate with very strong creative and computer science skills but little real-life business experience. Pairing that candidate up with someone in the business who is a strong strategic thinker and really understands the organization's needs is an excellent solution. Essentially, whenever you are looking to bring new people into the organization, focus on finding the balance of skills that works best for you. And, as with any position, the ability and desire to grow is incredibly valuable. Someone who doesn't tick all the boxes on paper but is very keen to learn new skills and grow with the business will always be a better fit than someone who is fixed in their ways and unwilling to learn – no matter how experienced or knowledgeable they are. The world of data is moving fast and new technologies and applications are emerging all the time, which means the ability to adapt and learn is becoming increasingly important.

Let's take a look at how Walmart recruits their data talent. Mandar Thakur, senior recruiter for Walmart's technology division, told me:

> We need people who are absolute data geeks – people who love data and can slice it, dice it and make it do what they want it to do. Having said that, there is one very important aspect we look for, which perhaps differentiates a data analyst from other technologists. It exponentially improves their career prospects if they can match this technical, data-geek knowledge with great communication and presentation skills.

In other words, as well as being able to wring critical insights from even the unlikeliest of data, they must be able to explain these insights to a room full of (often non-technical) business executives and marketing people. 'Someone who has this combination of skills can rise to the top very quickly', explains Thakur.

Most of Walmart's data recruits still come with a 'traditional' background in the academic disciplines required for data analysis – statistics, mathematics, computer science and business analytics. A working knowledge of Python or R, two of the programming languages most commonly used for analysing large data sets, is also usually expected. The biggest challenge can be finding candidates with experience in the most cutting-edge analytics applications, such as those involving machine learning. Many people will not have the opportunity to learn this at school, and experts are often self-taught. Another challenge is attracting talent away from Silicon Valley to Walmart's headquarters in Bentonville, Arkansas. To help with this, Walmart recently ran a recruitment campaign across social media using the Twitter hashtag #lovedata to raise its profile among the online data science community. They have also run crowdsourced data analysis competitions (see later in the chapter) and offered jobs to the most promising entrants. Referrals are another valuable source of job applicants – data fans are an active online community, so if you provide one with a great job, he or she is likely to spread the word to their peers.

Walmart also emphasizes the need to enhance recruits' business skills. Analytics and big data are now integrated into every vertical within Walmart, so, once on the team, every new staff member with these responsibilities takes part in the Analytics Rotation Program – spending a period within every department to get an overview of how analytics is used across the company. 'This allows them to combine their analytical knowledge – whether they have gained it in education or in work experience – and helps to assimilate that knowledge with what Walmart is doing in different pockets of their business', says Thakur.

Training and upskilling your existing staff

Rather than hiring data scientists with the five essential skills, you may be able to build on the skills that already exist in your organization and train your existing staff to fill any gaps. Therefore, as part of any data strategy, it's always a good idea to look at developing your existing people wherever possible. Just as with recruiting new staff, the key to successfully developing your existing people is to balance the understanding of the business itself with vital analytical and technical skills. This can be achieved in any number of ways – for example, you could train your business analysts in the use of big data tools.

Upskilling your workforce does require an investment in time, but it doesn't have to mean a large financial investment. Lots of universities are now offering courses in data science and there are many free online programmes available. One household name which is making waves in big data education is IBM. Its Big Data University initiative, with a range of free online courses, has now attracted more than 400,000 students. Students can sign up independently at home and work at their own speed. (However, IBM also works with partners to tailor course packages to fill the needs of individual organizations.) Although the Big Data University is owned and administered by IBM, it is considered a 'community' rather than a corporate division and its courses are designed to be fully platform agnostic. As Leon Katsnelson, IBM's director and CTO for analytic platform emerging technologies, told me, 'We teach people, we help people get skills, we are not there to teach how to use IBM products.'

Money is often seen as one of the biggest obstacles barring the way to education for many people and businesses, so IBM are not the only providers offering free online courses in big data and analytics. Increasingly, many colleges and universities are putting courses online where they can be studied for free. For example, The University of Washington's 'Introduction to Data Science' is available online at Coursera. It covers the history of data science, key techniques and technologies such as MapReduce and Hadoop, as well as traditional relational databases, designing experiments using statistical modelling, and visualizing results. Harvard has also made its 'Data Science' course available for free online. In addition, Stanford has a 'Statistics One' course, which is also available on Coursera. Many data science courses require a basic knowledge of programming, so familiarity with a programming language like Python will be helpful. Luckily, Coursera, Codecademy and MIT all offer free courses in Python designed for absolute beginners. There are also free online courses in data visualization, such as UC Berkeley's 'Visualization' course which is available through the UC Berkeley website.

Wherever possible, you should be looking to improve the ability to analyse data across the whole business – meaning rather than relying on just a few people to turn data into insights, you should make it as easy as possible for a wide range of people in the business to analyse data and use it to inform their decision making. There is an ever-growing plethora of tools and services designed to facilitate big data analytics outside of the IT lab and across the organization as a whole, giving rise to the term 'citizen data scientists' – non-data scientists with some degree of data science skills. In fact, the need for citizen data scientists has been forecast to grow five times more quickly than the need for people specifically trained as data scientists.

In Chapter 3, we saw how retailer Sears recently empowered 400 staff from its business intelligence (BI) operations to carry out advanced, big data-driven customer segmentation – work which would previously have been carried out by specialist big data analysts – creating hundreds of thousands of dollars worth of efficiencies in data preparation costs alone. Sears used tools provided by Platfora to allow its BI staff to effectively retrain and repurpose themselves as big data analysts. Platfora VP of products Peter Schlamp told me:

> Customer segmentation is a very complex problem. It is not something your average Excel user can do. There was a gap between needing a data scientist – a really highly trained scientist who can do [big data-derived] segmentation – and an analyst, which they had a lot of. Their goal was to enable a new class of user – citizen data scientists – from a group of business intelligence analysts. And by doing this they have been able to make better decisions about what products are being shown to users as they use their websites.

This isn't to say that businesses no longer need educated and experienced data scientists, it just means that data is becoming more democratized. And this is a good thing. After all, achieving 'buy-in' across the organization has often been put forward as a major obstacle that data projects have to overcome. What better way to overcome this obstacle than empowering a greater number of people to work with data?

Outsourcing your data analysis

When it isn't possible to upskill your staff or hire new people, or when you need to supplement your in-house capabilities, you will need to consider outsourcing your data analysis. There is a large market of data providers out there who can handle your data and analytic needs – and the market is growing all the time. Whether you're looking for an all-in-one service covering everything from collecting data to presenting key insights (see big data as a service in Chapter 8), or you just need some help with analysing data you already have, there will certainly be a provider who can meet your needs. Some data providers even specialize in specific sectors and industries, such as retail or banking. When it comes to third-party providers, hiring a big data contractor is usually the most common option. However, if you don't want to be locked in with a specific provider, you might consider crowdsourcing your data analytics. I look at both options below.

Partnering with a data service provider

Some of the biggest data providers are household names, like Facebook, Amazon and IBM, but you certainly aren't limited to the big corporations. There are plenty of smaller contractors out there and these may provide a more personalized, tailored service or have specialist knowledge of your industry. In fact, in my experience, industry-specific providers are becoming the norm as opposed to big generalists. While the big-name providers may have enormous data sets and impressive armies of analysts at their disposal, they aren't necessarily the best option if your strategy requires very specific information.

Unfortunately, the data industry isn't regulated or accredited in the same way as other professional industries such as accounting and insurance. Therefore, when looking for a third-party provider, it's a good idea to start with recommendations from your networks and contacts wherever possible. Failing that, there are many data case studies available online and in books (including my own book *Big Data in Practice: How successful companies used big data analytics to deliver extraordinary results*[4]), and these help to highlight providers who are doing excellent, innovative work. Also consider whether specialized knowledge of your business sector is important or not as that will inform the selection process.

I would say the five key data skills set out earlier in the chapter are just as applicable when seeking to hire a third-party provider, and they should at least serve as a basis for discussions. Creativity and business skills, for example, are just as important as analytical skills if you're looking to get the very most out of data. It's therefore vital you partner with a provider who understands what you're trying to achieve in the business. The better your contractor understands your key business questions, your strategic goals, and the challenges you face as you work towards those goals, the more likely they are to get to the insights you really need. Always ask for examples of who the provider has worked with in the past – even if you have read about their work in case studies or they have been recommended to you by a trusted contact. You will want to find out as much as possible about how their previous projects unfolded, what the key challenges were, and, crucially, what *concrete results* the clients saw as a direct result of working with that provider.

Finally, wherever possible, it's a good idea to have your draft data strategy in place before you approach data providers. It's important to nail down what you're trying to achieve with data before you can find the right partner to help you achieve that.

Remember Dickey's Barbecue Pit from Chapter 2? The restaurant chain serves as a great example of successfully partnering with a data provider. The company has a full-time IT staff of 11 people, including two dedicated analytical staff, but they also work with a data partner, iOLAP. iOLAP delivered the data infrastructure behind Dickey's big data operation and works closely with the company in their ongoing use of data for improved decision making. In Dickey's experience, finding people with the right data skills and convincing them to apply those skills to the world of barbecue was quite a challenge. 'There is a huge skills gap in the market compared to need. For us, part of the challenge is not only finding folks with the right skill sets – it is convincing them that barbecue really is doing big data', says Dickey's CIO Laura Rea Dickey. In this instance, partnering with an external provider helped supplement the company's in-house talents and plug those skills gaps. As Dickey told me:

> Even though our team is probably a bit larger than the traditional in-house team for a restaurant business – because it's where our focus is – it requires a partner. We have been very lucky in choosing the right partner. We have an account contact in our office at least 20 hours a week and we're working very closely with them at all times – it's closed the gap of what would have been a skills shortage for us if we didn't have a partnership like this.

This is another useful consideration when selecting a data provider – how much time can you expect with the contractors on a weekly basis and how will they work with your existing team?

Kaggle: crowdsourcing your data scientist

We know that companies around the world are finding that there is a serious shortage of trained data scientists, and demand for talent outstrips availability (at least for now). Could crowdsourcing data analytics provide part of the solution? Kaggle, the crowdsourced data analysis competition platform, certainly thinks so. Essentially, Kaggle acts as a middleman: companies and organizations bring their data (whatever it may be), set a problem to solve as well as a deadline, and offer a prize. Then Kaggle's army of armchair data scientists compete to come up with the best solution. It's a fascinating idea which has so far seen contestants compete to solve problems ranging from analysing medical records to predict which patients are likely to need hospitalization, to scanning the deep cosmos for traces of dark matter. Chief scientist of Google – one of the many companies that have used Kaggle's services – Hal Varian has described Kaggle as 'a way to organize the brain-power of the world's most talented data scientists and make it accessible to organizations of every size'.

The San Francisco-based company was founded in 2010, inspired by a competition organized by Netflix the previous year. The streaming TV and movie company had challenged the public to come up with better algorithms to predict what their customers would like to watch next, to help them improve their own recommendation engines. Netflix have since gone on to use Kaggle to organize their later competitions, again demonstrating just how successful the platform has been.

The data is generally simulated, to avoid privacy concerns around the companies passing on confidential information or commercially sensitive data that could fall into the hands of competitors if offered on a public platform. And as for the analysts themselves, anyone can register with Kaggle and enter most of their competitions. However, certain competitions are reserved for 'masters': site members who have proved their mettle in previous competitions. The prize is usually cash, but not always; some businesses have offered permanent jobs to competition winners.

When Walmart came to Kaggle with a data problem, they offered a job rather than a cash prize. As Mandar Thakur told me:

> The supply and demand gap is always there, especially when it comes to emerging technology. So we have found innovative and creative ways to go about finding talent for our data science and analytics teams. We're always looking for top-notch talent who can come in, contribute and catapult us even further.

For the Walmart competition, entrants were provided with simulated historical sales data from a number of stores, along with dates and details of promotional events, such as sales and public holidays, which it was thought would influence the sales of the item listed. Candidates were tasked with producing predictive models showing how the event schedule would affect sales across each of the departments where sales data was available.

As a result of the first competition, held in 2014, several people were recruited into Walmart's analytics team, and the competition was held again the following year in the hope of finding more. (In the second competition, candidates were asked to predict how weather would impact sales of different products.) One of the winning entrants, Naveen Peddamail, is now employed at the retail giant's Bentonville, Arkansas headquarters as a senior statistical analyst. He told me:

> I already had a job with a consultancy, so was really just browsing Kaggle as a hobby. I saw the Walmart challenge and thought I would give it a try. I thought I'd try to do some predictive analytics. After preparing and submitting my model, I ended up among the top entrants and was invited to meet with Walmart's analytics team.

Knowing that communication skills and other business skills are as important as analytical skills, Walmart had to factor this into their recruitment process. Therefore, the top-performing competition entrants, having proved their skills in raw analytics, were invited for further assessment at the company's headquarters. The jobs were eventually awarded to those who showed a clear ability in reporting and communications as well as analytical talent.

Thakur says there were other benefits aside from filling vacancies for both Walmart and the analytics community at large: 'Kaggle created a buzz around Walmart and our analytics organization. People always knew that Walmart generated a lot of data but the best part was letting them see how we use it strategically.'

Other competitions on the site challenge entrants to predict which customers are most likely to respond to direct-mail marketing campaigns, using simulated personal data, identifying physics phenomena using data from CERN's Large Hadron Collider, and predicting categories of crime that will be committed in San Francisco, using demographic and historical crime data.

Kaggle shows that great data scientists can come from anywhere. They will not always have a formal educational background in statistics, mathematics or computer science, as is generally expected. The analytical mindset can be developed in many areas of life. Indeed, for Walmart, the crowd-sourced approach led to some interesting appointments of people who, as Thakur says, wouldn't have been considered for an interview based on their resumes alone. One candidate, for example, had a very strong background in physics but no formal analytics background: 'He has a different skillset – and if we hadn't gone down the Kaggle route, we wouldn't have acquired him.'

Crowdsourcing has great potential for identifying emerging talent and it provides businesses with new ways of engaging with people who can potentially help them solve their problems and answer key business questions. And because the competitive element ensures those taking part will strive to make sure their ideas stand out from others, this encourages out-of-the-box thinking that can lead to some very innovative solutions for businesses. So, if you are struggling to attract talent or, for whatever reason, you don't want to partner with a data provider, then it is certainly worth considering crowdsourcing your data analysis. It's a great way to supplement skills, access additional analytical brainpower, and test the waters on new data projects.

Endnotes

1 Josh Bersin, Jason Geller, Nicky Wakefield and Brett Walsh (2016) Human capital trends report 2016, *Deloitte Consulting*, 29 February, available at: https://dupress.deloitte.com/dup-us-en/focus/human-capital-trends/2016/human-capital-trends-introduction.html

2 Thomas H Davenport and D J Patil (2012) Data scientist: the sexiest job of the 21st century, *Harvard Business Review*, October issue, available at: https://hbr.org/2012/10/data-scientist-the-sexiest-job-of-the-21st-century

3 Bernard Marr (2016) Is being a data scientist really the best job in America? *Forbes*, 25 February, available at: http://www.forbes.com/sites/bernardmarr/2016/02/25/is-being-a-data-scientist-really-the-best-job-in-america/#648ede7f5f98

4 Bernard Marr (2016) *Big Data in Practice: How successful companies used big data analytics to deliver extraordinary results*, Wiley, Chichester

Ensuring your data doesn't become a liability: data governance

10

We know that businesses are collecting and analysing ever-increasing amounts of data as they try to make better decisions, run their operations more efficiently, and increase profits. Companies of all sizes are investing in data in a big way and many believe their huge data depositories are turning into one of their biggest business assets. And they're right. But there are some significant hurdles around data ownership, privacy and security which must be overcome for any business to get the most out of data. Ignoring these issues, or failing to properly address them, could see data go from a huge asset to a potentially lethal liability. Collecting and storing data, especially personal data (which, let's face it, is what a lot of business data is) brings serious legal and regulatory obligations. Falling foul of these can have disastrous consequences for your businesses reputation as well as leave you exposed to costly lawsuits.

Sadly, too many organizations overlook these key issues. Until recently, there has been something of a Wild West feel about big data. Companies have been able to collect whatever data they like, for whatever reason (often no good reason whatsoever), with very little oversight. As we'll see in this chapter, all that is starting to change and regulations are being introduced to tighten up how companies collect, store and use data. Therefore, it is vital any organization factor data ownership, privacy and security issues into their data strategy. Proper consideration of these issues (as well as others outlined below) comes under the umbrella of 'data governance'. In this chapter, I explore some of the key considerations around data privacy, ownership and security, and define what good data governance should look like in any organization. Keep in mind that these are all large topics, each worthy of books in their own right, and the regulatory landscape is changing. Specialist legal advice is therefore recommended.

Considering data ownership and privacy

We appear to be entering the end of the Wild West data collection era, where companies can collect as much data as possible without thinking about why they want it and how they'll use it. Now, data ownership and privacy considerations must be a key priority for companies working with data, especially if it's personal data. There are two strands to data ownership: one is making sure you own any data that is essential to your business, as opposed to relying on a data provider, and the second is ensuring the correct rights and permissions are in place that allow you to use that data in the way you intend.

To own or not to own?

Many businesses do brilliant things using third-party data, and the wealth of data providers mean that even the smallest company can benefit from data. This is, of course, a good thing. However, if your key business processes are going to be based on certain data or if you intend to monetize data, it is very important to own that data, rather than rely on a third party's supply of data. When data becomes a part of your core everyday operations or revenue stream, the business starts to rely on that data and it becomes a vital part of how you do business. It stands to reason then that you would own any data that your business relies upon. As I've said throughout this book, it's important to think of data as a core asset, just like your employees, your intellectual property, and your inventory.

Make sure that, wherever possible, you own the data that is crucial to your business operations, revenue, or even critical decision-making processes. This is easy enough to ensure when working with your own internal data, but it is admittedly less straightforward with external data. If you can't gather your own external data and you turn to a third-party provider, you need to make sure that you at least aren't going to lose access to the data. If you're reliant on a third party's data, and the supplier ups their prices or denies access for any reason, it could mean serious disruption to your business.

Ensuring the correct rights are in place

Whether you're using your own data or data that you have purchased from elsewhere, you must ensure the correct rights are in place that allow you to use the data in the way you intend. Metadata, which includes crucial information like when and where the data was collected, and what permissions were granted, is extremely helpful in this respect. Many companies don't worry about having (or if they do have it, updating) this critical metadata, especially if they have purchased data from a supplier. It's not uncommon, for instance, for a business to purchase customer data in a large database and have no real idea where this data came from and what permissions were granted at the time. In my experience, companies don't ask for the vital metadata nearly as often as they should. As laws around data and privacy tighten up, it will become increasingly difficult for any business to use data without this metadata information. Therefore, if you're purchasing a data set, you must be able to trace that data back to its origins in order to understand when it was collected, from where, and with what permissions. It's like a responsible publisher knowing where the paper used in its books was sourced from, and how that precious resource is managed.

The General Data Protection Regulation (GDPR), an EU regulation which comes into force in 2018, is designed to enhance data protection for individuals and give them greater control over their personal data and how it is used. The new regulation means firms can face heavy fines (up to €20 million or 4 per cent of annual worldwide turnover) for misusing or inadequately protecting personal information. As a general rule of thumb, private data has to be protected and can only be used *for the purpose for which it was handed over*. Therefore, when collecting your own data, you must tell users what data you are collecting and how you intend to use that data, and then take steps to ensure the data is not used for any other purpose. If you want to use the data in a different way, fresh permission is required.

As Ashley Winton, a partner in the corporate law firm Paul Hastings, told me, you will also need to ensure that any bought-in data has been cleared for use by the people who are selling it. As the end user, it is your responsibility to ensure you are not misusing data, even if you purchased that elsewhere. In other words, if you buy a list of names and addresses to use for marketing purposes, and it turns out that the person who sold you those names and addresses didn't secure the right permissions when they collected them, it's you that will end up facing fines from regulators and potentially ruinous lawsuits from people whose data you have misused. Again, this is where having accurate metadata can prove incredibly valuable.

In the United States, regulation around the use of personal data may be less stringent, but there are still many things that can trip a company up. Felix Wu, professor of law at the Benjamin N Cardozo School of Law, told me, 'Unlike Europe, the US does not have comprehensive privacy regulation, but this may actually make things more difficult for companies, which must comply with a patchwork of varying state and federal laws.'[1] One area in which the United States does regulate more substantially is around issues involving deception, Professor Wu tells me:

> Companies can run afoul of laws against deception without even intending to deceive. This means that companies need to keep track, in a detailed way, of what their data-handling practices are – including what they collect, how they use the data and to whom the data is disclosed – in order to ensure that their practices are consistent with what they say in their privacy policies, marketing materials and elsewhere.

Professor Wu highlights Google as a relevant example of a company which has been tripped up by collecting data which was 'useless to the company'. The search giant has landed in legal hot water over collection of private data by cars capturing images (and WiFi data) for its Street View service.

Data minimization as good practice

Even when we're talking about 'big' data, there is great value in a 'less is more' approach. With regulations tightening up, the days of big corporations collecting every speck of data they can just in case it proves useful one day (or as Jeff Bezos, CEO of Amazon, put it, 'We never throw away data') are gone. Not only is this an expensive approach, since the more data you collect, you more you will have to invest in data storage and analysis, it may land you in legal trouble.

The new EU GDPR insists that any personal data collected must be 'adequate, relevant and limited to the minimum necessary for the purposes for which the data are processed'. In effect, this means collecting and holding only the minimum amount of personal data needed to fulfil your purpose. This is exactly what is meant by the term 'data minimization', or limiting the collection of personal information to that which is directly relevant and necessary to accomplish a specified purpose.

Particularly as the IoT continues to grow, organizations are faced with more and more ways to collect more and more kinds of data, including (and especially) private, personally identifiable data. While some companies may still hope to save all this data for some future application, the dangers of data hoarding are similar to those of physical hoarding: mounds of useless junk that make it very difficult to find what we need when we need it. It costs money and time, and can become dangerous. Instead of a 'save everything' approach, any good data strategy should embrace a data minimization policy, keeping only what you really need. Even a data giant like Walmart only relies on the previous four weeks of data for its day-to-day merchandizing strategies, demonstrating that it is possible to run a very successful business with a data minimization approach.

Personally, I feel very strongly that companies should only collect and store the data they really need, and delete everything else. Storing data 'just in case' is a dangerous (not to mention expensive) path.

All data storage costs money, and no business has an infinite budget – so no business can go on collecting and storing data indefinitely. In addition, too much data (especially personally identifiable data) brings big risks. The consequences of data loss and breaches must be considered, too. A major leak of sensitive personal information can easily destroy a business's reputation or even lead to charges of criminal negligence. You can imagine how much more galling this would be if you didn't even need the data that you lost in the first place!

With the implementation of the GDPR, all businesses that hold data about any European Union citizen will need to make data minimisation standard operating procedure to minimize risk. I see this as an entirely positive move, both for individuals and for companies.

Understanding privacy concerns

Legislation is also tightening up around individuals' right to privacy. The GDPR shores up the right for individuals within the EU to be forgotten, which means individuals can ask companies to delete their personal data and the companies have to comply. This may not sound like a big deal, but consider the implications of deleting every trace of a customer from your systems. Do you have procedures in place for deleting customer data? How many systems would be affected? Can you be sure you're removing all trace? Do your people understand how important it is to comply with this regulation? These are all things that need to be considered as part of your data strategy.

The right to be forgotten, the need for data to be *relevant*, and other issues around privacy makes companies like Facebook and Google, and indeed any company that has built its business on gathering mountains of personal data, quite vulnerable. One interesting recent case involving Google demonstrates this. In 2015, Daniel Matera, who is a non-Gmail user, filed a lawsuit against Google, alleging that the company has violated the Wiretap Act by intentionally intercepting and scanning e-mails sent to or received from contacts with Gmail accounts for the purpose of targeted advertising.[2] He maintains that, as a non-Gmail user, he has not given consent for Gmail to intercept his e-mails and is therefore not subject to Google's privacy policy. Google, on the other hand, argued for the complaint to be dismissed because intercepting and scanning e-mails is part of its everyday business, and it is these practices that facilitate targeted advertising – which, in turn, allows Google to offer its e-mail services free of charge. The judge, however, rejected Google's argument on the basis that intercepting and scanning e-mails is not intrinsically necessary to delivering them. Google's motion to dismiss the complaint was denied and the next step is for the court to rule whether the lawsuit meets the requirements for a class action – which would allow a whole 'class' of consumers to join the case. If this goes ahead, and if Google is found to have infringed these consumers' privacy rights, the compensation bill could be hefty indeed.

Google has always argued that users of its free e-mail service can't legitimately expect privacy, but continuing to extend this to anyone who has any contact with Gmail users will be tricky in a climate of increasing regulation and litigation. Personally, I would always recommend to my clients that they are open and transparent about the way they collect data. Clearly, Google is providing a useful and free service, and we all know the company has to make money somehow. The issue is that many of the Gmail users will not even be aware that this is what they have signed up for (let alone anyone who corresponds with them) because most people simply click 'accept' without ever reading or understanding any privacy policies. Likewise, in Chapter 2 we explored the huge backlash against music streaming service Spotify's privacy policy, which was questionably broad regarding what data was being collected, what it would be used for, and whom it would be shared with.

There were similar privacy concerns around the launch of Windows 10 in 2015.[3] Many of the concerns stemmed from the fact that, if users follow the software's recommendations and stick to default settings while installing their free upgrade, they are effectively giving Microsoft permission to directly monitor pretty much everything they do on their machines. What's more, many users – perhaps unknowingly if they are complacent about reading privacy policies – give Microsoft permission to share this information with unspecified 'partners', and for unspecified reasons. Windows 10 is clearly designed to learn as much about users as it can. Most consumers are used to the idea of software providers gathering data on how we use their products, particularly in cloud-based services. But Windows 10 goes beyond that by also automatically assigning an advertising ID to every user so that, based on their data analysis, Microsoft can tailor ads in their web browser and other applications.

It is possible, if you diligently check all of your privacy settings, to make sure you are retaining some level of control over what is sent to Microsoft and their partners. However, doing so will disable some of the selling-point features of the new OS, such as Cortana, the voice-driven, artificially intelligent personal assistant. Cortana will not operate without access to your location and permission to transmit a lot of other usage data back to Microsoft. However, it's fair to say that none of this is specific to Microsoft. Mobile computing is as popular, if not more so, than PC-based computing these days, and both of the major mobile OS's collect huge amounts of data on our usage and share it with their providers and partners. Interestingly, though, such large-scale mobile data scooping has generally caused less concern.

Pokémon Go, the wildly popular augmented reality game, is another example of how sweeping privacy policies and terms of service can come across as, frankly, sinister. The game uses your smartphone's camera, GPS, and position sensors to tell the game what to display and where, creating the illusion that cute little cartoon 'pocket monsters' are standing in your living room, on the street outside, or in the park nearby. You grab free Pokéballs (to catch the critters) at local sites of historical interest. And businesses can purchase Pokémon 'lures' as advertising to draw imaginary monsters and real fans to their physical location. The game is insanely popular. In fact, it is fast becoming the most successful mobile app of all times, having been installed by 6 per cent of all Android devices in the United States at the time of writing. At this rate, it is likely to surpass Twitter in terms of the number of daily active users.

But the way the phone app works requires data – and lots of it – and problems have arisen with what the app collects, and what the company is doing with it. News began to percolate that the game required full access to your Google account when you sign in. Full access allows the app – and the company behind it – to 'see and modify nearly all information in your Google account', according to Google's privacy controls. It doesn't have access to passwords or payment information, but it can read your e-mails, see what you've been searching for, and more.

The company, Niantic, said the request was a mistake and has reportedly changed the access requirement in updates to the game. But the fact remains that so many users were happy to give a game designed for 10-year-olds full access to everything Google knows about them. It is yet another example of how people give away their data far too easily. Especially with apps, where we download something for free and want to start using it quickly, people never read the lengthy terms of service agreements they're happily agreeing to, and don't understand the full extent of the information they're voluntarily giving away. The problems I see exemplified by the recent concerns over the Pokémon Go app – and others like it – are twofold.

First, companies are in a land grab to collect as much data as possible about their customers against current and potential future use scenarios when it will become valuable. Most are taking the road of forcing savvy users to opt out of this data collection, rather than allowing them to opt in, as program features require the information.

Second, and perhaps more importantly, users are blissfully ignorant about the privacy they're giving up every time they click the 'accept' button on a new app or program. Not until some interested computer scientist, journalist, or hacker discovers the distasteful truth is there any kind of outcry. I believe responsible companies should implement common-sense policies and terms of service that are easy for customers to understand, particularly when it comes to what personal data they are giving away and why.

In general, most people are happy to give companies access to certain data if it allows them to benefit from a valuable service for free or receive a better service or product – but only on the basis that they know what they're giving up and why. Nobody likes being duped, or feeling as though they've been duped, as recent backlashes have shown. Therefore, companies should no longer take it for granted that users will simply tick the box on the privacy agreement and think no more about it.

Naturally, all this applies to data on your employees, just as much as your customers or users. Companies have more data on staff than ever before and data analytics is fast becoming a routine part of HR practices. As the world becomes increasingly digital, companies have endless ways to monitor their staff.

My fear is that many companies will spend too much time crunching all the things they can so easily collect data on, including how much time employees sit in their office chairs or how many people they have interacted with, rather than the more meaningful qualitative measures of what they did when sat in the chairs and the quality of their interactions with others. It is therefore prudent for companies to follow the same data minimization practices with employee data as they would with customer data, and gather only that which is necessary, ie data that can help meaningfully improve company performance. Employees will also need to be made aware of what data is being collected, why, and what the company will use it for – ideally with a positive tone that emphasizes the benefits of this data. Just as hundreds of millions of people are seemingly happy for Google to scan their e-mails in return for a free e-mail service, your employees are more likely to be happy with you using their data if they understand that the information will be used to improve their working environment, for instance.

There's certainly a lot to consider in terms of data ownership and privacy, but I'm not trying to put you off. With transparent privacy policies and good data governance processes in place (see later in the chapter), and by keeping abreast of the latest regulations, there's no reason why any business shouldn't successfully use data. The key takeaways here are to remember that whenever you ask individuals for their data, it is imperative you explain what data you require, what you intend to do with it, and whether you might share that information with anyone else (again, this is only advisable if it is necessary to the intended purpose). This should also be on an 'opt in' basis, ie don't automatically gather and use data unless the user opts out; rather they should expressly opt in and give permission for you to use their data. Likewise, when purchasing personal data from a supplier, it is your responsibility to ensure that this was properly explained to the individuals concerned and that they have given the appropriate permissions. And, of course, you should practise data minimization and only ever gather data that is necessary to your business, never on a 'just in case' basis.

Tackling data security

Your data strategy should also take account of data security considerations, ie the need to prevent data loss and breaches. When you consider data as an asset, you need to take its security very seriously, just as you would with other assets like your business premises and inventory. There have been many high-profile data breaches in the last few years and regulations are toughening up when it comes to data protection.

In short, any company dealing with personal data 'by which an individual can be identified' is responsible for its protection. This means even if you purchase personal, identifiable data from a data provider, you could potentially be held responsible for any data breach. Thus, wherever possible, it is a good idea to use anonymized data that doesn't identify individuals' details. When this isn't possible, you need to take measures to ensure the data is secured. (Even if this isn't a legal requirement in your country, there can be huge reputational consequences if customer data is breached.) There are certain safeguards any business can put in place to secure data and prevent data breaches. Such measures can include encrypting your data, having systems in place to detect and stop breaches while they are happening, and training your staff so they never give away secure information.

Keep in mind that data security is a specialist field and it is always a good idea to consult with a data security expert when developing a data strategy, particularly when weighing up the pros and cons of various data storage methods and data security systems.

The huge impact of data breaches

Data breaches can lead to huge losses for business, in terms of legal costs and financial compensation, as well as the damage done to a company's reputation. Sadly, data breaches are becoming more and more frequent and it seems like barely a week goes by without reports of yet another large-scale loss or theft of personal data.

Perhaps this is inevitable. The total volume of personal data we generate and store is increasing exponentially as more and more aspects of our lives become digital and connected. So it follows that with more data floating about, more of it will be stolen or lost. From a business point of view, however, this increase is significant. According to a recent study, the cost to a business of dealing with an 'average' data breach is now US $4 million.[4]

A scan of the headlines on any given week will usually uncover various incidences where credit card numbers and addresses have been stolen. But, as inconvenient as incidents like these are, these consequences pale into insignificance when compared to the potential carnage that could be caused by data breaches in the future, given the amount of information that is now being shared online. Several data and privacy experts have been willing to admit that they see the potential for a 'perfect storm' data breach on a scale that could have seriously damaging social consequences. And one of the defining consequences would be a terminal loss of confidence among the public in sharing information online.

Often, nothing more than user names and passwords are stolen, as in recent large-scale hacks on Tumblr and Myspace. (However, even this can have serious consequences if, as is often the case, users have used the same user name or password on other, more sensitive services.) Sadly, more serious data breaches are becoming more common. The Identity Theft Resource Center lists over 400 serious data breaches known to have taken place in the first seven months of 2016 alone.[5] They involve organizations as diverse as the Bay Area Children's Association (a counselling and mental health non-profit), the National Network of Abortion Funds, and the University of New Mexico Hospital. Considering the kind of information organizations like this may hold, the ramifications of a serious data breach clearly go beyond the financial or political – there can be serious social consequences.

What is really worrying is the possibility of an attack on the scale of the Myspace or Tumblr hacks, against a target with very socially sensitive data. Two possibilities that have been touted are leaks of personal message data from Facebook, or user data from Google. There is certainly no suggestion that there's an imminent threat of a breach at either company but it is interesting to consider how devastating the ramifications could be.

When considering the possibility of a large-scale leak of messages from Facebook or a similar socially focused data set, we can of course look to the 2015 Ashley Madison hack as a precedent. It's fair to say that this was the first time the public at large may have become aware of the potential social consequences (as opposed to financial or political consequences) of poor data security. The fact that Ashley Madison's data set was particularly salacious guaranteed it plenty of press attention. And it certainly had some very real consequences for those who were exposed as cheaters, as well as for their families. Anyone not involved was able to reassure themselves that they wouldn't have been affected by this because they weren't using a service designed for adulterers. But the consequences could be far more severe with a more 'mainstream' service like Facebook. I would feel safe betting that a far greater volume of infidelity is carried out over Facebook private messages than on Ashley Madison. Infidelity aside, countless other deeply private, personal and potentially damaging conversations also take place via Facebook messaging. Sensitive conversations about individuals' employment, or activist activity, religious beliefs and social activity take place every second of the day. Most worryingly, in the majority of cases, these conversations are linked to a definite, real, verified name of a person.

If the idea of having everything you have said in private conversation over the last 10 years uploaded to the Internet, linked to your real name, and compiled into a searchable database isn't terrifying enough, imagine the same thing happening with the data Google collects on us. Google stores each and every search query we make (whether or not we are using private browsing or signed into an account), often tied to a real name or, if not, then tied to an IP address which will pretty much show Google who it belongs to.

This is really information which you don't want to fall into the wrong hands. Google has dedicated itself to learning how to build profiles of people from the information they input into its services. In reality it has done this by conditioning us to enter as much data as we possibly can. Our phones constantly report our location. Speech recognition systems store recordings of our vocal commands which can be analysed for insight into our emotional state and stress levels after they have filled their primary purpose of letting us tell Google what to do. And in the near future, Google's autonomous cars will send real-time sensor data from wherever they go. When you consider that they could – either by design or through the intervention of third parties – identify individual people they pass in the street by communicating with mobile phones in the vicinity, you can't help but picture it as a surveillance network which will potentially be on a scale beyond anything we have seen in the past. The possibility of a data set such as this existing at all may be scary enough for many of us, but the consequences of it falling into the wrong hands could be catastrophic.

Of course, there are also good reasons to be confident this won't ever happen. Hackers would have to have technological capabilities beyond those they have today to bypass security on the scale that is deployed by Google or Facebook. The fact that hacks of the type I imagine here haven't happened yet is evidence of that. Additionally, in the case of a hack on a global scale like this, significant resources would be needed to host and share the data. Just about 25 gigabytes of user data has so far been distributed from the Ashley Madison hack – a small enough volume that it can easily be shared using BitTorrent. A hack on the scale I describe here would likely involve petabyte-scale volumes – a far more difficult prospect to host and make available to the public, particularly while retaining anonymity. But just considering the implications of a data leak on this scale is enough to make any business leader take data security extremely seriously.

Considering IoT threats

The IoT and its ever-expanding network of connected devices present an extra layer of security concerns. The notion that computers need to be kept secure is now pretty much commonplace. Even your grandmother is probably comfortable running a virus checker on her home PC these days. But it takes a stretch of the imagination to understand that attacks could soon be coming from a multitude of other angles. With the explosion in IoT devices, users and businesses are inevitably becoming more vulnerable to hacking. Many are now arguing that the same levels of precautions that apply to computers should also apply to smart devices.

The theory is simple – more devices mean more possible attack vectors for intruders who want data. The how and the why is a bit more complicated – what benefit would an attacker gain from taking control of a smart TV? Well, aside from causing mischief (which is certainly the main motive for a good deal of IoT hacking activity) the likelihood is that they want to use it to take advantage of network vulnerabilities which would allow them to get at the real jackpot – other devices such as PCs or phones which are far more likely to hold sensitive and valuable information.

Another angle of attack would be faked faults and prompts to make service calls or download patches. These patches could be malware designed to access other devices on the network through the supposedly faulty appliance. Ransomware is another potential danger. These viruses are already used to infect computers and make valuable data unusable unless a ransom is paid. Last year researchers at Symantec showed that this sort of virus could be programmed to spread from one device to another, locking the user out of their phone, then their watch and, in the future, perhaps their car, fridge or entire house.[6]

Internet-connected cars, toys and even medical tools have already been shown to be vulnerable to attack. And new vulnerabilities are being found every day, as quickly as manufacturers can patch them. Any company dealing in IoT-related devices needs to take their security very seriously.

Again, you need to make it clear to users what data you will be collecting from devices and why, so that they can make an informed decision on the potential risks and benefits. You should also firmly encourage users to always, always change the default password on their connected devices. In addition, carefully consider just how connected devices really need to be. If you manufacture a smart thermostat, for instance, it makes sense for this to connect to the user's phone. But the ability to connect to the smart fridge or TV? There's little tangible benefit to this extra level of connectivity.

From a software perspective, you will need to stay up to date on the latest threats and regularly update your product with fixes to counter these threats. And users will need to be educated on why these updates are important. You must also make sure you choose any partners very carefully, particularly any third-party supplier who might be hosting data on your behalf. The reputation of your suppliers could have a direct impact on your own organization's reputation.

It also makes sense to practise data minimization with IoT devices. The 'collect it all and analyse it later' mindset should be a thing of the past – it's a strategy which poses far too many risks. Any piece of personal data which can potentially leak or be stolen should be thought of as a security risk both to your company and the consumer, particularly in light of the forthcoming legislation.

Practising good data governance

So far in this chapter we've uncovered a lot of pitfalls to working with data. How do you make sure you avoid these pitfalls? The answer lies in comprehensive data governance policies. Data governance refers to the overall management and caretaking of data, covering its usability and integrity (ie making sure the data is of a good quality, that you know where it has come from and that you have the right to use it as you need), and security.

Data governance means you should be aware of the moral and legal requirements and regulations concerning every step of your data operations, and have firm policies and procedures in place to govern every step. Good data governance is of course about making sure you're not breaking any laws, that you have the correct permissions and metadata in place; good practice is to include the metadata with the data itself, making explicitly clear what permissions and governance apply to that particular bit of data. Data security is also an obvious part of a data governance framework. But data governance goes further than data security, ownership and privacy; it extends to having policies in place to determine exactly who has access to data, and who is responsible for maintaining the quality and accuracy of that data. A big part of good data governance relies on building a data culture within your organization, and I talk more about this in Chapter 11. Essentially, at every layer of the organization there should be a culture of data being the foundation of good decisions and efficient business operations, and there should be a company-wide impetus to take care of data and treat it as the valuable asset that it is.

Your data governance plan should define who is the owner of various data within the organization and who is accountable for various aspects of the data. Consider, who is responsible for data accuracy (which may be everyone who comes into contact with it if you adopt a data stewardship approach like we saw in Chapter 8)? Who is responsible for maintaining access to the data and controlling who can access it? Who is responsible for updating the data? A good data governance programme should also set out clear procedures for how the data can be used, especially if your company deals with personal data.

Naturally, your data governance programme should ensure the company is compliant with regulations, and set out procedures for maintaining this compliance, such as regular audits. As we've seen in this chapter, legislation is certainly tightening up when it comes to matters of use or misuse of personal data, and fines can be enormous. So it is becoming more important than ever to make sure you are compliant with every piece of legislation that affects you. If not, it's only a matter of time before what should be one of your business's biggest assets becomes one of its biggest liabilities.

There are many other steps you can take to ensure you have thorough data governance procedures in place. For example, if you collect images from CCTV for analysis, notices should be in place making it clear what that data is likely to be used for. If you use Bluetooth or Apple's iBeacons to capture data about customers on your premises from their mobile phones, the agreements that they give which allow you to collect this data must explicitly state what it is used for. And if you buy in data from a third-party supplier, it is absolutely essential to check the fine print to see what conditions were given to the supplier when they collected the data.

Who is responsible for data governance? It makes sense to have a specific resource or team that's responsible for planning, implementing and maintaining data governance. Theoretically, this could sit within a range of departments from IT to business operations or policy departments, but it must always include a high level of input from business leaders and appropriate data stakeholders across the company. You might, for example, like to appoint data stewards across the organization who are tasked with coordinating with the data governance team and maintaining data quality across their various departments.

At its heart, data governance is about managing data as one of your business assets. Just as you have processes and systems in place to facilitate managing your staff, the same applies to your data. By putting a strong data governance framework in place as part of your data strategy, you are paving the way for successful and *safe* use of data. Your customers and employees, indeed all business stakeholders, will thank you for it.

Endnotes

1 For more on my conversation with Professor Wu see Bernard Marr (2016) Big data: how a big business asset turns into a huge liability, *Forbes*, 9 March, available at: http://www.forbes.com/sites/bernardmarr/2016/03/09/ big-data-how-a-big-business-asset-turns-into-a-huge-liability/2/#1e869be11f5e

2 For an overview of the privacy case against Google see Kat Sieniuc (2016) Google can't escape Gmail privacy suit, judge says, *Law360*, available at: http://www. law360.com/articles/828337/google-can-t-escape-gmail-privacy-suit-judge-says

3 For more information about the Microsoft Windows 10 privacy concerns see Conner Forrest (2015) Windows 10 violates your privacy by default, here's how you can protect yourself, *TechRepublic*, 4 August, available at: http://www. techrepublic.com/article/windows-10-violates-your-privacy-by-default-heres-how-you-can-protect-yourself/

4 IBM (2016) 2016 cost of data breach study, available at: http://www-03.ibm. com/security/data-breach/

5 For an up-to-date list of data breaches, see the Identify Theft Resource Center website at: http://www.idtheftcenter.org/2016databreaches.html

6 Bernard Marr (2016) 5 simple steps to protect yourself from IoT security threats, *Forbes*, 3 May, available at: http://www.forbes.com/sites/bernardmarr/ 2016/05/03/5-simple-steps-to-protect-yourself-from-iot-security- threats/#51fffe0774ff

Executing and revisiting your data strategy

11

Creating a robust data strategy is one thing, but it must also be properly executed across the organization. Successful data strategy execution relies upon every layer of the company buying into the data strategy and understanding the importance of putting data at the heart of decision making and business operations. Business leaders should be looking to create a strong data culture across the company, with data being recognized as a key business asset. But a data strategy is not carved in stone – especially when you consider how fast the technology around data and analytics is moving. Instead, a good data strategy should evolve as new technologies are discovered and as the business's needs change. Therefore, you should revisit and renew your data strategy on a regular basis to ensure it meets the business's ongoing needs and challenges. In this chapter I look at each of these aspects in turn, from putting the strategy into practice to creating a data culture to revisiting the strategy.

Putting the data strategy into practice

When I work with clients, this is probably the one phase that I find most rewarding, because it's about turning data into *action*. After all, having a data strategy, making infrastructure investments, and collecting and analysing data is all meaningless unless you can turn data into action – be it better decisions, improved business operations, increased revenue, or all three. When you put a data strategy into practice, you are making a commitment to improving, or even transforming, your business – and that's an exciting thing to be involved in.

Attitude is key

Proper execution of your data strategy has to start at the top of the organization, just as it would with any other business-critical strategy. Senior leadership must buy into the idea that data is a vital part of how you run the business and create revenue, and how people across the organization make decisions. With senior leadership buy-in, you can create a top-down ripple effect, where the notion of data as a core asset filters through every layer of the organization.

There are several attitudes I encounter regularly that can kill a big data strategy faster than anything else. Identifying and neutralizing these attitudes is key to getting the strategy off the ground and into implementation:

- 'We are not a data company.'
  I'd argue that every company is now a data company. Data is everywhere and a part of everything, and I cannot think of a single industry or business that couldn't benefit from understanding more about their customers, their sales cycles, demand for their product or service or their production inefficiencies.

- 'It's too expensive.'
  This is a flat-out myth because those on a tight budget can get started by using relatively cheap cloud services and open-source software.

- 'We already have more data than we need.'
  It is true that most companies are already overwhelmed by the amount of data in their business and the thought of collecting more fills many business leaders with dread. However, the proliferation of data means that there are so many new data sources we can use and, what's more, many of those data sets can be accessed for free. The trick is to drill down to the data you really need, as opposed to a 'collect everything' approach.

- 'Everyone else is already ahead of us.'
  You may feel your competitors are way ahead but putting your head in the sand now is not going to make it any better in the future. Besides, even though more companies than ever are working with data, many are still in pre-implementation or pilot stages. In other words, you might not be as far behind as you think.

- 'Our customers aren't asking for it.'
  If your customers are looking for things like a more personalized service, comparative pricing, optimized supply chains or flexible maintenance

cycles, they're asking for the things that only data can help you deliver. And the hard truth is, if you don't provide it, someone else will.

These are just a few of the negative attitudes I've encountered when someone at the top is uncertain about implementing data technologies. These misconceptions can only be overcome with education and concrete examples of how data can benefit business. I've given a number of examples throughout the book, but you may also like to seek out examples from your specific field to really hammer home the advantage of putting data into action in your business.

Why data strategies fail

The principles of executing a data strategy are broadly the same as any other strategy. Your data strategy acts as a roadmap for what you are looking to achieve and what you need to put in place for that to happen, including data collection methods, analytic tools, infrastructure investments, and hiring new talent or upskilling your existing workforce. It is a plan to get from point A to point B, whatever those points may be for your company. A strategy is a series of actions, after all, but it's also a vision of where the company is heading. Depending on the scale of your data strategy, you may need to break the strategy down into a number of smaller projects, making it more manageable and easier to oversee. Whether you do this or not, you will certainly need milestones and a timetable to mark critical steps in the implementation, such as having your data collection and analytics systems in place, testing systems before they go live, and training staff on any dashboards or visualization tools. These steps will need to be 'owned' by individuals or teams, with clear lines of responsibility. And obviously, as with any project, progress needs to be carefully monitored to ensure the implementation remains on track. There's an old saying that 'what you measure, grows', but I find the opposite is also often true – projects left unmonitored go nowhere.

Unfortunately, many companies fail to execute their data strategies successfully. Sometimes the strategy itself may not be achievable, or it may be so vague or ill-defined that no one knows where to start. In my experience, this is mercifully rare. In any case, the chapters in this book are designed around the core requirements of a good data strategy (such as deciding how you want to use data), ensuring you cover everything you need to in a way that is achievable for your organization.

Communication, or lack of it, is another big stumbling block. Often strategies are not communicated effectively, so nobody understands them. When managers and employees who are charged with implementing various elements of a data strategy don't understand how the pieces fit together and how it benefits the business, they are less likely to care about the implementation. Sometimes a little context is all that's needed to help a strategy succeed. When people are told to do X, with no reason why, they don't see a need to do it, so they don't do it. If, on the other hand, they are shown why X is important to the business, they're much more likely to see that it gets done. In turn, the strategy is more likely to succeed. This brings us back to the issue of buy-in, and how important it is to strategy implementation. Yes of course senior leadership must buy into the data strategy, but so must managers and employees across the company. If employees are not party to the thinking behind a strategy, they may not agree with it or even believe in it. This can result in lacklustre performance or low morale. It is also important that employees feel they have a voice in the strategy implementation. One way to address this is to provide space for everyone, at every level, to contribute to strategy execution, perhaps through an internal company blog with open comments, or an intranet communications platform where people can discuss the implementation.

In Chapter 1, we learned about Royal Bank of Scotland's 'Personology' strategy, which aims to bring the bank back to 1970s levels of customer service. RBS's head of analytics, Christian Nelissen, told me that getting staff on board with the new strategy was absolutely critical to its success:

> We're at the point where the staff feel like they are having valuable conversations with their customers. They're at the point where they understand what the data is trying to do and feel it helps them have good conversations – and that's a big shift from where we were before. Staff engagement is critical – the ideas that work best, and that have the best resonance with customers, are the ones that we either got from the front line or we developed working really closely with the front line.

Lack of communication between departments can also be an issue. One study found that just 9 per cent of managers say they can rely on their counterparts in other departments all of the time.[1] This may be because people in different departments don't know one another well or even feel like they are part of the same team. If this is true in your company, the implications for your data strategy could be duplicated efforts, delayed deliverables, and missed opportunities. Therefore, regular cross-departmental communication is vital when your data strategy is on the line. It's important for every department to understand how they and everyone else fit into the bigger picture, as well as who is responsible for what. The same applies to communication between the organization's data staff and those elsewhere in the organization. To get the most out of data, data functions need to be able to communicate successfully with other departments and leadership, and vice versa. With this in mind, you should look to build and maintain strong links between whoever is analysing the data, whoever is reporting the insights, and business leads. Indeed, a recent survey found that just 41 per cent of participants thought that this collaborative relationship between data and business executives exists at their company.[2] Diving deeper into the figures, among 'leading' companies, this figure rose to 55 per cent. This highlights how improving communication between data functions and business leaders can be critical to a company's success.

Management failure can also seriously impede or even kill a data strategy. I admit, this is something of a catch-all and it is in no way unique to a data strategy, but particularly if your data strategy is very resource-intensive, management failure can have disastrous consequences. Sometimes it's because those holding the purse strings haven't taken into account some long-term or ongoing cost associated with the strategy, or sometimes senior managers don't trust the algorithms – many got where they are today on gut instinct and they aren't going to start letting a computer tell them what to do now. Mismanagement can come from many angles and the UK National Health Service's fatally botched National Programme for IT is a prime example. The plan to bring all patient medical records into a central database was described as the 'biggest IT failure ever seen' and was scrapped after more than £10 billion (US $14.9 billion) had been spent.

Just as fatal can be not having the right skills at the right time. Companies are often fond of starting data projects without thinking enough about how this might impact resources in the future. And, as we saw in Chapter 9, skilled data science staff are in limited supply and some out-of-the-box thinking may be required. For example, one of my banking clients told me that, while they have a lot of business analysts, they aren't trained in big data and aren't really data scientists. We identified the key skills gaps and developed a customized course to move people from being business analysts to becoming big data scientists, which was significantly cheaper than hiring a new team of data scientists. In addition to the training, the bank looked to universities and colleges, which often offer the service of students or academics to provide analytical support to businesses.

It's clear that there are quite a few stumbling blocks that commonly hinder data strategies, and this certainly isn't intended to be an exhaustive list, but with strong communication and a high level of buy-in across the company, you're well placed to implement your strategy successfully.

Creating a data culture

Essentially, getting buy-in across the company is about creating a data culture. In a data culture, data is recognized as a key business asset, and it is used, wherever possible, at every level of the business to make improvements – whether this means better business decisions, a better understanding of your customers, more targeted marketing efforts, a more efficient supply chain, new revenue opportunities, and so on. As much as possible, the whole business should be using data as the basis for what they do. This is not an easy thing to achieve as it clearly requires a culture shift away from gut-based decisions, or the 'this is how we've always done it' mindset.

There's no doubt that the shift to a data culture must be driven by those at the top and cascade down through every layer of the organization. Those at the top must lead by example and use data as the basis of what they do. If the leadership make a commitment to basing decisions and the way the business is run on data, then those below will follow. It sounds obvious but it is so important to *use* the insights that data gives you – you really need to act upon the insights found if you are to encourage others in the organization to do the same. If you do nothing, you have no hope of shifting overall company culture. So use those precious insights, demonstrate positive outcomes, and it will be much easier to get buy-in from others.

A good way to sow the seeds for a strong data culture is to engage key personnel in the data strategy, both in developing the strategy and in its implementation. For example, if you are using data to better understand and target your customers then you would clearly involve your marketing lead from the outset. You want those key personnel to become data advocates, creating a trickle-down effect through their departments.

A data culture is about everyone across the business understanding the *value* of data and how it can help the business succeed. Communication is therefore key. Leaders and managers should spend time engaging people in the data strategy, stressing how it will benefit the organization and its employees and customers. It's a good idea to use examples from other companies to demonstrate the positive impacts of data, either using examples from this book or specific case studies from your industry.

Change can be difficult for many people and businesses, and negativity is contagious. If certain individuals or teams are particularly resistant, use their 'pain points' to show how data can improve their working environment or make their job easier (by making it easier to run successful marketing campaigns, or reducing customer complaints, for example). Focusing on the positive outcomes certainly helps smooth the way.

Finally, you should, as I have emphasized many times in this book, be open with your employees about what you're measuring and why, especially when it comes to employee data. Big data does have certain 'Big Brother' overtones that can make people nervous. Don't avoid the issue. People are far more likely to be comfortable with data if you're honest about what data you're gathering and the positive impact this will have.

Implementing a cultural shift in an organization, whether it's a small business or a large corporation, is not a quick and easy job. It takes time and dedication to get company-wide buy-in and it requires a shift in mindset away from gut-based decisions or the 'this is how we've always done it' mentality. But it is crucial if you're to get the very most out of data. The result will be a smart, efficient company that leverages data successfully and continuously looks to improve the way it does business.

Revisiting the data strategy

As with any good strategy, you need to regularly review and revise your data strategy. There are two strands to consider: one is how the data and analytics technology has moved on, and the other is whether your business needs have changed. In both cases, you need to ask yourself, 'What does this mean for our data strategy?' When you think of data as a business asset – as important as your product, your employees, and so on – it makes sense that it requires careful monitoring and regular reviews, just as with other key business assets.

If you are using data to improve your decision making or business operations, I recommend conducting a full revision of the data strategy once a year as part of your regular annual planning cycle. However, if your business model is based on data (ie you are monetizing data), you may have to review more frequently than once a year. Essentially, how often you review and revise your strategy will be based on how important data is to your business, what sort of data you're using and what you're trying to achieve with data – but an annual full review is a sensible rule of thumb.

Changing business needs

No business is set in stone. Goals change, markets evolve, and new commercial opportunities arise. Therefore, how you want to use data in five years' time, or even two years' time, may be different to how you want to use data now. Your data strategy needs to be able to evolve and shift with your business's needs. Say you're using data to improve decision making and you start off with a list of critical business questions. Some of the strategic questions you're asking will be one-offs; some will be around ongoing issues that you want to continue to measure and monitor. And some of the answers you discover may lead to entirely new questions that you want to explore in future. As such, your data strategy will evolve in line with your new business questions.

Or you may start this journey in one area of your business, and then extend it to other areas of the business that can also benefit from data. If you're using data to optimize your delivery routes, for example, a logical next step might be to use sensors to monitor vehicle wear and tear and automate vehicle maintenance schedules. Once you have the data infrastructure in place, it's relatively easy to extend the applications to other areas of the business. But you will need to thoroughly renew your data strategy to ensure you are considering all the potential impacts and requirements.

You may even find that the data itself points to a new business opportunity that requires a significant overhaul of your data strategy. John Deere is just one example of a company that found incredible value in the data its agricultural machines were collecting, leading to a whole new business model for what was once a very traditional manufacturer. As with much of business, the trick is to stay open to any new opportunities.

The changing technology landscape

The exciting thing about data is that things are changing all the time, although this naturally presents a challenge for businesses who are trying to keep up. Collection methods and analytics technology in particular are moving very fast, and companies who do not revise their data strategy in line with new developments risk being left behind. I'm not suggesting any business throw out their existing infrastructure and jump on new technology bandwagons once a year, but it is nonetheless important to consider new advancements and whether these have any impact on your data strategy. One positive aspect of the changing technology landscape is that it can actually drive infrastructure costs down; for example, storage options are increasing and getting cheaper all the time, so regularly reviewing your strategy could point to valuable cost savings.

We explored some of the key technology advances in Chapter 1, including blockchain technology, machine learning, the IoT, affective computing, virtual reality, cognitive computing and robotics – these are all areas in which the technology is evolving quickly. 'Edge analytics' is another critical development to keep an eye on. Sometimes known as distributed analytics, edge analytics basically means designing systems where analytics is performed at the point where (or very close to where) the data is collected, eg a smartphone or other smart, connected devices. Often, this is where action based on the insights provided by the data is most needed. So, rather than designing centralized systems where all the data is sent back to your data warehouse in a raw state, where it has to be cleaned and analysed before being of any value, why not do everything at the 'edge' of the system? A simple example would be a massive-scale CCTV security system, with perhaps thousands or tens of thousands of cameras covering a large area. It's likely that 99.9 per cent of the footage captured by the cameras will be of no use for the job it's supposed to be doing – eg detecting intruders. Hours and hours of still footage is likely to be captured for every second of useful video, so what's the point of all of that data being streamed in real time across your network, generating expense as well as possible compliance burdens? Wouldn't it be better if the images themselves could be analysed within the cameras at the moment they are captured, and anything found to be useless either discarded or marked as low priority, freeing up centralized resources to work on data of actual value?

It's a model which is increasingly being rolled out across industries – a recent IDC FutureScape for IoT report found that by 2018, 40 per cent of IoT data will be stored, processed, analysed and acted upon at the edge of the network where it is created.[3] While edge analytics is not intended to entirely replace centralized analytics, it's particularly helpful in cases where businesses need to react very quickly or in real time to what the data is telling them.

Large retailers, for example, could analyse point-of-sales data as it is captured, and enable cross-selling or up-selling on the fly, while reducing bandwidth overheads of sending all sales data to a centralized analytics server in real time. Or emergency repair work and equipment downtime can be reduced when manufacturers build edge-based analytical systems into machinery and vehicles, allowing them to decide for themselves when it is time to reduce power output.

Autonomous and driverless vehicles will heavily rely on edge analytics systems for functions that require immediate response, such as hazard avoidance. At the same time, they will rely on centralized analytics for fleet management and optimization of pathfinding. They will also rely on a middle ground, sometimes known as 'the fog', with analytics being carried out between a network of vehicles which are close together, for the purpose of managing local traffic flow. The smart approach is to process data at the most efficient place, whether it's the edge of the network or in a centralized resource, or somewhere in between.

In short, the principle that makes edge analytics such an enticing prospect is that it means bringing the analytics to the data, rather than the other way around. As data sets grow ever larger, and IoT-enabled devices grow ever smarter, it is likely that it will become an increasingly important part of data strategies.

Another development to keep track of is LiFi. The enormous demand for WiFi and transmission of mass quantities of data is putting a strain on the current technologies. LiFi, a method of data transmission more than 100 times faster than traditional WiFi, could provide the answer – and it only requires that you turn on a light. LiFi is a category of Visible Light Communication, using LED lights which flicker at speeds undetectable to the naked eye to transmit data – a bit like high-tech Morse code. In fact, scientists have demonstrated in a lab that they can transmit information at as much as 224 gigabits per second, the equivalent of 18 movies of 1.5 gigabytes each being downloaded every single second.

One massive advantage is that the LED lights require so little energy, they can be powered by a standard ethernet cord. In addition, LiFi does not create electromagnetic interference the way WiFi does, meaning it could have important applications in sensitive locations like healthcare facilities. There are drawbacks, however. In very bright daylight, the receivers wouldn't be able to distinguish the signal, and unlike WiFi, LiFi signal cannot pass through walls. Of course, these limitations could be overcome with technologies like smart architecture where the light follows the user around the space. And actually, the fact that LiFi cannot pass through walls makes the data stream instantly more secure; users must be physically in the space in order to access the data.

As the market for IoT devices grows and sensors are added to more and more things and places, faster and heavier data transmission will be required. Our current infrastructure simply cannot handle the quantity of data that will need to be transmitted if the IoT continues to grow at predicted rates. LiFi (or something like it) may be the only viable solution if we want big data and the IoT to continue to grow. Best of all, because existing LED lightbulb technology requires only the addition of a tiny microchip to become a LiFi transmitter, eventually, the more than 14 billion lightbulbs in the world could be converted into 14 billion LiFi transmitters.

Looking even further ahead

There are also developments on the more distant horizon that may have a significant impact on how organizations use data. In Chapter 1, I explored how advances in robotics and AI may lead to drastic changes in people's jobs, and even cause many people to lose their jobs. These advances will naturally have an impact on business models and everyday operations as well. The truth is, no one knows for sure where the world of data and analytics is heading in the more distant future, but let's explore a couple of possible future scenarios.

While improvements in machine learning, artificial intelligence, big data and robot automation could mean huge advances in medicine, science, commerce and human understanding, it's also undeniable that there will be consequences as well. These technological advances represent a significant challenge to capitalism. Together, they are poised to potentially create jobless growth and the paradox of an exponentially growing number of products, manufactured more and more efficiently, but with rising unemployment and underemployment, falling real wages and stagnant living standards.

But what if the prognosis weren't all doom and gloom? What if all this automation were instead to provide so much luxury that we enter a post-work era, when humans are required to do very little labour and machines provide everything we need? This is the theory of 'Fully Automated Luxury Communism', the idea that, in the not-too-distant future, machines could provide for all our basic needs, and humans would be required to do very minimal work – perhaps as little as 10–12 hours a week – on quality control and similar oversight. Instead of creating even further inequalities, it could lead to a society where everyone lives in luxury and where machines produce everything. (Think of the egalitarian society of The Federation portrayed in Star Trek where physical needs are met with 'replicators' and other advanced technology, and you have a pretty good idea what this theory is all about.)

The idea of a luxury communist utopia isn't exactly new. Obviously, the robots are new, but historians can trace the original idea back as far as the 19th century. The tricky part is subordinating the technology to global human needs rather than profits. But this has been the sticking point for communism since its conception. Without profits – or some other strong inherent incentive – what motivation is there to innovate, to adapt, to improve?

That isn't to say I think the idea is all bad. Putting modern technology to work for the people is an excellent goal. It is a worthy cause to bring governments and non-profit organizations onto the same technological footing as for-profit companies, and this could result in huge strides towards improving living conditions, decreasing crime, ending poverty and other problems.

For me, there's no question we're entering a new era of human development. Experts and futurists will argue endlessly about whether we're entering the Anthropocene, an age in which creativity is the driving force (like agriculture and industry have been before), or a technology age, in which technology is the driving force. If the latter, we face an uncertain culmination to all this advancement. Will technology be the great equalizer or continue to widen the gap between the digital haves and have-nots?

'Digital feudalism', where the tech-elite control and rule the world, is a worrying concept – both for individuals and businesses. Feudalism says that power rests with those who control the means of production. In the middle ages, that meant the kings and nobility who owned the land. In the industrial revolution, it meant the people who owned the factories and, eventually, the governments who controlled and regulated them. If we are indeed entering an age of digital feudalism, then the lords will be those who control the technology that the rest of us rely on.

It's already happening, to some extent. If you want the latest app, the latest gadget, you *must* agree to the company's terms. If you don't, you cannot use their technology. They control it. We are headed towards a future when it may be nearly impossible for the average person to 'opt out'. So far, public backlash against this has been surprisingly minimal, but it may take just one large-scale security breach, similar to those I explored in Chapter 10, to change this. In light of this, responsible companies should take great care to not force users to give up data that they aren't comfortable giving up. If we are entering an age of digital feudalism, the companies that allow their customers and users some measure of control may be those who come out on top.

All this is not intended to present a negative vision of a future where we're all slaves to our data. There is no doubt that our world is increasingly being driven by data, but this presents incredible opportunities for businesses who plan accordingly and create a robust data strategy.

With data, organizations can understand more about their customers than ever before, and provide a better service that is more targeted to the customer's individual needs. Data can help companies run their operations more efficiently, reduce waste, improve staff morale, and create better products. And let's not forget that smart products are not only a winner for the companies that sell them, they help make consumers' lives much easier. Data is also enabling increasing numbers of companies to evolve their business models and create whole new revenue streams that would not have been possible 10 years ago. It's an exciting time for businesses of all shapes and sizes, and data is at the heart of it.

Endnotes

1 Jolynn Shoemaker, Amy Brown and Rachel Barbou (2011) A revolutionary change: making the workplace more flexible, *Solutions*, March issue, available at: https://www.thesolutionsjournal.com/article/a-revolutionary-change-making-the-workplace-more-flexible/

2 Bernard Marr (2016) Why investments in big data and analytics are not yet paying off, *Forbes*, 27 June, available at: http://www.forbes.com/sites/bernardmarr/2016/06/27/why-investments-in-big-data-and-analytics-are-not-yet-paying-off/#6e42088580a2

3 IDC Futurescape (2015) Worldwide Internet of Things 2016 predictions, available at: https://www.idc.com/research/viewtoc.jsp?containerId=259856

INDEX

Acxiom 75–76, 77, 121
PersonicX system 76
Adams, D 38
advanced analytics: machine learning, deep
learning, cognitive computing
(and) 42, 75, 114–17 *see also*
machine learning
Amazon (and) 17, 28, 33, 34, 66, 73, 85, 91,
92, 97, 146 *see also* Bezos, J
Kiva Systems 61
optimised warehousing 60–61
Web Services 121, 127, 129, 130
analyses *see* analytics, types of
analytics, evolution of 102–03
analytics, types of 103–14
advanced *see* advanced
analytics
business experiments 107
cohort analysis 112
correlation analysis 108–09
data mining 106–07 *see also subject
entry*
factor analysis 112–13
forecasting/time series analysis 110–11
image 105
linear programming 111–12
meta analytics/literature analysis 114
Monte Carlo Simulation 111
neural network 113–14
regression analysis 109
scenario analysis 109–10
sentiment/opinion mining 104–05
text/text mining 103–04
video 105–06
visual 108
voice 106
Ancestry.com 74, 133–34
Apache Software Foundation 126, 127
Apixio: cognitive computing firm and
electronic health records
(EHRs) 92–93
Apple 73
iPhone 79
Watch 79, 93
artificial intelligence 57
automation, jobs under threat from 13–14

Bezos, J (CEO, Amazon) 154
big data (and) 1–2, 3, 26–27, 86–87

defining as volume, velocity, variety,
veracity – the four Vs 86–87
healthcare 4
life on Mars 3
as a service (BDaaS) 119, 120–22
skills shortages 138–39
*Big Data in Practice: How successful
companies used big data
analytics to deliver extraordinary
results* 146
building data competencies (and) 137–50
the big data skill shortage 138–39
building internal skills and competencies
(by) 140–45
essential data science skills *see* data
science skills
recruiting new talent *see* talent,
recruiting new
training and upskilling existing
staff 144–45
outsourcing your data analysis (by)
145–50
Kaggle: crowdsourcing your data
scientist 147–49
partnering with a data service
provider 146–47

Caesars Entertainment and use of data
analytics 45–46
Total Rewards Scheme 46
census data 92, 99, 123
CERN Large Hadron Collider 149
chief data officer (CDO) 17–19
core qualities of/requirements for 18
Cincinnati, Ohio 12
and Industry 4.0 demonstration city 12
citizen data scientist 51
cloud computing 8, 86, 102–03 , 119, 126
Coca-Cola 7, 75, 78
cognitive computing 5–7, 114–16
Watson system (IBM) 6, 115
competition, understanding 24
creating technology and data infrastructure
(and) 119–35 *see also* data
analysing and processing data *see* data,
analysing and processing
'big data as a service': one-stop
solution? 120–22 *see also* big
data
collecting data 122–24 *see also* studies

providing access to data (by) 132–35
    communicating data 134–35
    considering data stewardship 133–34
storing data 124–29 see also data
        storage systems
crowdsourcing 28–29, 150 see also Uber
    and Kaggle 147–49
customer behaviour 23–24, 40, 42
customer segmentation 11, 51, 145

data, analysing and processing (and) 129–32
    Amazon Web Services 130
    Cloudera CDH 130
    Hortonworks Data Platform 130
    IBM Big Data Platform 131
    IBM Watson 131
    Infobright 130
    MapR 131
    Microsoft HDInsight 131
    Pivotal Big Data Suite 131–32
    Splunk Enterprise 132
    three steps for 129
    tools and software for 129–30
data, social media platforms as sources of 98
data analytics/big data analytics 9–10, 45–46,
        51, 65, 76, 131, 145–47, 158
data collection 122–24 see also sourcing and
        collecting data
data governance 151–66
    data ownership and privacy 152–59
        see also subject entry
    practising good 163–65
    tackling data security 159–63
data mining 13, 106–07
    Oracle 140
data ownership and privacy (and) 152–59
    data minimization as good practice
        154–55
    ownership vs third party data
        supply 152
    privacy concerns and legislation 155–59
    rights and data protection 152–54
    tackling data security 159–63 see also
        data security
data – revolutionizing the world of business
        (by) 7–16
    automation and threat to jobs 13–14
    blockchain technology 15–16
    key uses of data in business 8–11
    and smart factories and Industry
        4.0 11–12
'Data Science' free online course
        (Harvard) 144
data science skills 140–42, 146
    analytical 140
    business and communication 140

computer science 141
    creativity 141
    and diversification of skillsets 141–42
    statistics and mathematics 141
data scientist(s)
    role of 138
    as 'sexiest job of 21st century' (Harvard
        Business Review) 138
data security 159–63
    hacks and breaches 161
    impact of data breaches on 160–62
    and IoT threats 162–63
data storage systems 124–29
    cloud-based/distributed 125–26
    and data lakes vs data warehouses
        128–29
    Hadoop 126–28 see also Hadoop
        storage system
    and security 126
    Spark/Spark Streaming 127–28
data strategy, executing and revisiting
        (and) 167–79
    creating a data culture 172–73
    putting data strategy into practice see
        data strategy in practice
    revisiting and data strategy 173–78
data strategy, revisiting (and) 173–78
    changing business needs 173–74
    changing technology landscape 174–76
    digital feudalism 178
    looking further ahead 176–78
data strategy in practice (and) 167–71
    creating a data culture 172–73
    negative attitudes, identifying and
        neutralizing 168–69
    reasons for failure of strategies 169–71
        lack of communication 169–71
        lack of skills 171
        management failure 171
    revisiting the strategy see data strategy,
        revisiting
data types, newer 93–96
    activity 93–94
    conversation 94–95
    photo and video 95
    sensor 95–96
data visualization, free online courses
        for 144
Davenport, T H (analytics expert) 107
deciding your strategic data needs
        see strategic data needs
decision making 13, 22, 37, 152 see also
        strategic data needs
deep learning 6, 57, 70, 78, 114–17
Delker, J (Pinsight) 41–42, 52
Dickey, L R (CIO) and 25, 52, 147

Dickey's Barbecue Pit and data system: Smoke Stack 24–25, 52, 85, 147
'digital feudalism' 178
Domino's 77, 132
    Information Management Framework 10–11
driverless vehicles 6, 175
Dunnhumby 75, 78

edge analytics/distributed analytics 174–76
Ek, D (CEO, Spotify) 35
employment: jobs under threat from automation 13–14
endnotes for
    building data competencies in your organization 150
    creating the technology and data infrastructure 135
    data governance 165–66
    every business now a data business 19
    executing and revisiting your data strategy 179
    sourcing and collecting data 100
    using data to improve your business decisions 55
    using data to improve your business operations 71
    your strategic data needs 36
European Union (EU) 155
    General Data Protection Regulations (GDPR, 2018) 153, 154, 155
every business as data business, reasons for 1–19 *see also* chief data officer (CDO)
    cognitive computing and artificial intelligence (AI) 5–7
    data as key business asset and key to competitive advantage 16–19
    starting with data strategy 16–17
    data as revolutionizing the world of business *see subject entry*
    growth of big data and Internet of Things 1–2
Etsy and Shop Stats system 132–33
executing and revisiting your data strategy *see* data strategy, executing and revisiting
Experian data analysis 76–77, 97
    and socio-demographic tool Mosaic 76

Facebook 2, 6, 10, 17, 23, 33, 42, 46, 73, 80–81, 93, 102, 127, 146, 155, 162
    buys facial recognition firm Face.com 78
    buys Instagram 82–83

Graph API Application Program Interface 98
    and Oculus Rift (VR headset) 55
facial recognition technology 6–7
finance, key questions related to 44–46
Fitbit 32–33
Ford: Synch in-car entertainment system 10
Fortune 500 companies 82
    ten most valuable 73
    using Hadoop 127
The Fourth Industrial Revolution 12
fraud 61–63
Fully Automated Luxury Communism 177

Google 17, 33, 34, 157, 162
    AdSense 121
    AdWords 121
    Alphabet 73
    Analytics 360 suite 53
    Apps for Work 32
    buys DeepMind 78
    Data Studio 53
    lawsuit: alleged violation of Wiretap Act 155–56
    Nest 80
    and performance of managers 50
    self-driving cars 6
    street view technology 116
    Trends 92, 99
    user data and storage of queries 161
Gordon, G (Kronos) 139
GPS data 26, 41–42

hacks and message leaks 161–63 *see also* data security
Hadoop storage system (Apache Software Foundation) 103, 126–27, 130, 131, 144
    and Cloudera 127
The Hitchhiker's Guide to the Galaxy 38
human development and the Anthropocene age 178

IBM (and) 15, 97, 146
    Analytics for Twitter 121
    Big Data University 144
    Predictive Analytics 140
    Slamtracker statistics interface 133
    Twitter 23
    Watson analytics 43
    Watson Health 79
    Watson platform and healthcare 67–68
    Watson system 6, 115
    The Weather Company 31, 74
    Wimbledon 133

Industry 4.0 11–12
Instagram 82–83
International Data Corporation 16
International Institute for Analytics 16
Internet of Things/Everything (IoT/IoE) 5,
        57, 154
    and blockchain technology 15
    threats to 162–63
'Introduction to Data Science' (University of
        Washington) 144

John Deere 78–79, 121, 133
    Farmsight 67
    myjoindeere.com 67
    services 67

Kaggle 147–49
Katsnelson, L (IBM) 144
key areas of organization: customers,
        markets and competition; finance;
        internal operations *and* people 38
key business questions (related to) 37–50
    customers, markets and competition
        40–43
        and how data provides insights –
            Pinsight *and* Wimbledon
            (2016) 41–43
        finance 44–46
    and good questions – better answers
        38–40
    internal operations 46–48
    your people 48–50 *see also* Google
Kodak 82–83
Krowitz, A (Kronos) 139

Laney, D (Gartner) 32
Lifi data transmission 176
LinkedIn 32, 74, 93
loyalty cards 3, 4, 74–75

machine learning 57, 114–17
    and ability of machines to see, read,
        listen, talk and write 116–17
machine-to-machine (M2M)
        communication 135
Macy's (US) 65, 75
MapReduce 127, 129, 130, 144
marketing 23–24
Matera, D (allegation of violation of Wiretap
        Act, lawsuit against Google
        2015) 155–56
Microsoft 4, 7, 15, 73, 117, 156–57
    buys LinkedIn 32, 74
    Cortana 116, 157
    HealthVault 32

Twitter bot 6
    Windows 10 and privacy concerns 156
MIT 144
MIT Technology Review 33
monetizing your data (and) 73–83
    data as core business asset 74–77
    increasing value of your organization 74
    selling data 78–82
    understanding value of user-generated
        data 82–83
    value of company's ability to work with
        data 77–78
Monte Carlo Simulation 111
Myspace 160–61

Narrative Science 63–64
Nelissen, C (Royal Bank of Scotland) 170
Netflix 3, 91, 148

Oracle Data Mining 140

Pareto principle (80/20 rule) 44
Peddamail, N (Walmart) 149
Persado natural language software 14
'personology' strategy (Royal Bank of
        Scotland) 170
Platfora 145
Pokémon Go reality game 157–58
    and Niantic 157
predictions 5, 6, 26, 107, 110, 113, 115
predictive models/modelling 12, 29, 62–63,
        91, 141, 148–49
privacy 17, 18, 32, 34–35, 42, 98, 148, 151,
        152–60, 164, 165
programming languages 129, 138
    Python 143, 144
    R 143
project performance 47
projects, failure of 47

Qlik and Narrative Science partnership 54
QlikView 134
Quill (Narrative Science) 54

ransomware 163
Rattenbury, T (Trifacta) 141–42
reports (on) data scientists (Glassdoor,
        2016) 138–39
    future of blockchain technology (World
        Economic Forum) 15
    IoT data (IDC Futurescape for IoT) 175
research showing virus spreading between
        devices (Symantec) 163
risk assessment 63
    and Monte Carlo Simulation 111

robotics 11, 57, 61, 71, 174, 177
Rolls-Royce 59–60, 67, 85
    data-driven manufacturing success
        of 29–31
Royal Bank of Scotland (RBS): big data
        strategy 'Personology' 9–10, 170

Sanders, C (Ancestry.com) 133
SAS Analytics 140
scenario planning 109–10 *see also* analytics,
        types of
    as five-stage process 110
Schlamp, P (Platfora) 145
Schwab, K (founder of World Economic
        Forum) 12
Schwarz, M (Square Root) 139
Sears 51
    business intelligence (BI) operations 145
    and Platfora tools 145
sensor data 2, 11, 21, 34, 85, 87, 90, 93,
        95–96, 97, 162
sensors 4, 8–9, 11, 26, 27, 30, 39, 48, 57–
        60, 64, 67, 69, 79, 100, 121–24,
        133, 157, 174, 176
ShotSpotter technology 64, 124
Skype video conferencing 117
'smart cities' 68–69, 71
smart devices 4, 5, 8, 69–71, 162
Snelson, G (Milton Keynes Council) 69
sourcing and collecting data (and) 85–100
    accessing external data from companies,
        social media, government
        data sets 97–99
    gathering your internal data 96–97
    newer types of data 93–96 *see also* data
        types, newer
    non-existent data 99–100
        and Springg agricultural data
        company 100
    understanding different types of
        data 86–93 *see also* big data *and*
        structured data
Spark open source system 127–28
Spotify and privacy policy 34–35, 156
Sprint telecommunications 41, 42, 52
    subsidiary Pinsight Media 41–42
Stanford 'Statistics One' course 144
strategic data needs (and) 21–36
    importance of the *right* data 33–35
    making a strong business case 35–36
    transforming your business model: data
        as business asset 31–33
        to boost company value 31–32
        turning data into new revenue stream:
        Fitbit 32–33

using data for better business decisions
        (and) 22–25
    seeing data in action: Smoke
        Stack 24–25
    understanding customers and
        markets 23–24
using data to improve operations
        (and) 25–31
    Amazon: optimizing business
        processes to increase sales 28
    gaining internal efficiencies 26–27
    Rolls-Royce: data-driven
        manufacturing success 29–31
    Uber business model 28–29 *see also*
        crowdsourcing
structured data 88–93
    defining 88–89
    and defining external data 91–93
        internal data: downsides and
        upside 90–91
        unstructured/semi-structured
        data 89–90
Structured Query Language (SQL) 88, 102,
        119, 131
studies (on)
    cost of data breaches in US 160
    data: concern about governance and
        privacy (Gartner Research
        Circle) 32
    differentiating pro golfers from
        average golfers using big data
        (GolfTEC) 123–24
    risk of automation to existing jobs in UK
        (Oxford University) 13
supply chain(s) 12, 46, 116, 168, 172
    analytics 47–48
        real-life example of 48
    and delivery 26
    management 9, 60–61
survey on
    difficulties in finding talent to carry out
        analytics (2016) 138
    influence of knowing company
        performance on positive
        performance of employees (UK
        and US) 53

talent, recruiting new (and) 142–43 *see also*
        Walmart
    analytical skills 142
    enhancement of business skills 143
    programming languages 143
Tesco/Tesco Clubcard 74–75, 77, 78, 80
Thakur, M (Walmart Technology
        division) 143, 148, 149

Thomas, M D (SAS software architect) 54
tools
  Qlik 53
  Tableau 53, 134
toys, 'smart' 70
ToyTalk/Mattel and 'Hello Barbie' 70
Transport for London (TfL) 68, 124
trend spotting 23–24
Tumblr 160–61
turning data into insights (and) 101–18
  advanced analytics *see subject entry*
  combining analytics for maximum
    success 117–18
  different types of analytics 103–14 *see
    also* analytics, types of
  the evolution of analytics 102–03
Twitter 10, 23, 24, 42, 90, 93, 98–99, 143,
    157
  Tweets 23, 32, 87, 89, 98, 102, 121

Uber (and) 82
  and crowd sourcing 28–29
  Starwood Hotels and Resorts 81
United Kingdom (UK)
  Meteorological Office 99
  National Health Service
    National Programme for IT 171
    use of customer profitability
      analytics 45
  Transport for London 124
United States (US) (and) 157
  government: free availability online of
    government data 99
  The Identity Theft Resource Center 160
  National Climatic Data Centre 99
  regulation on personal data 153–54
using data to improve your business
    decisions (and) 22–25, 37–55
  questions related to customers, markets
    and competition (and) 40–50
    key finance questions 44–46
    related to internal operations 46–48
    related to your people 48–50 *see also*
      Google
  setting out key business questions 37–40
    see also key business questions
  visualizing and communicating insights
    from data (by/with) 50–55
    blended approach for access to
      data 51–52

combining visuals and words for
    maximum impact 53–54
  data visualization 52–53
  virtual reality and future of data
    visualization 54–55
using data to improve your business
    operations (and) 57–71
  optimizing your operational processes
    with data (and) 58–66
    enhancing business processes 61–64
      see also fraud
    enhancing sales and marketing
      processes 64–66
    enhancing warehousing and
      distribution 60–61
    improving the manufacturing
      process 58–60
  using data to improve customer offering
    (by) 66–71
    delivering better customer service
      67–69
    delivering better (and 'smart')
      products 69–71
    and 'smart cities' 68–69

Varian, H (Google) 148
virtual reality (VR) 54–55
Visible Light Communication 176

Walmart (and) 65–66, 92, 132, 148–49
  Analytic Rotation Program 143
  correlation analysis – Pop-Tarts and
    hurricanes 109
  recruitment of data talent 143
  Social Genome Project 66
  structured data 88
wearable technology 5
weather data 99
Weinstein, L S (TfL head of analytics) 68,
    124
Willis, A (All England Law Tennis and
    Croquet Club) 43
Wimbledon (2016) 42–43
Winton, A 153
WIRED magazine 82
World Economic Forum 12
Wu, F (Benjamin N Cardozo School of
    Law) 153–54

CPSIA information can be obtained
at www.ICGtesting.com
Printed in the USA
LVHW080110140519
617741LV00007B/18/P